"Sirah Vettese has written a v̶e̶r̶y̶ ̶i̶n̶s̶i̶g̶h̶t̶f̶u̶l̶ ̶—̶ love. She illumines both heart and mind."

> —**Marianne Williamson**, author of
> *A Return to Love* and *Illuminata*

"Sirah Vettese's writing shines with clarity, warmth, understanding and truth. Her insights into the nature of relationships will change your life."

> —**Deepak Chopra**, M.D, author of *Ageless Body, Timeless Mind*

"While written for women, this book offers both sexes valuable information about reclaiming their power, taking charge of their lives and ultimately creating a love that works."

> —**Susan Jeffers**, Ph.D., author of *Feel the Fear and Do It Anyway* and *Opening Our Hearts to Men*

"This is a very insightful book which helped me in my own marriage. I highly recommend it."

> —**Jack Canfield**, coauthor of *Chicken Soup for the Soul*

What Happened to the Prince I Married?

Spiritual Healing for a Wounded Relationship

By
Sirah Vettese, Ph.D.

Published by

Aslan
PUBLISHING

2490 Black Rock Turnpike, #342
Fairfield, CT 06432

Aslan Publishing
2490 Black Rock Turnpike, #342
Fairfield, CT 06432
Please contact the publisher for a free catalog of
other books by Aslan Publishing.
Phone: **203/372-0300**
Fax:: **203/374-4766**
E-mail: **info@aslanpublishing.com**

IMPORTANT NOTE TO READERS:

The suggestions in this book for personal and relationship healing and growth are not meant to substitute for the advice of a trained professional such as a psychologist or psychiatrist. The publishers and author expressly disclaim any liability for injuries resulting from use by readers of the methods contained herein.

Library of Congress Cataloging-in -Publication Data
Vettese, Sirah
What happened to the prince I married? : spiritual healing
for a wounded relationship / Sirah Vettese — 1st ed.
p. cm.
Includes bibliographical references.
ISBN: 0-944031-76-5 (pbk.)
1. Interpersonal conflict   2. Marital conflict.   3. Man-
woman relationships.   4. Man — Psychology.   5. Intimacy
(Psychology)   I. Title.
BF637.I48V48   1999
306.872 — dc21   98-28001
                                                CIP

Book design by Dianne Schilling
Cover design by Linda Hauck
Printing by Baker Johnson, Inc.
Printed in the USA
First Edition

I dedicate this book to my cherished and beloved prince, Harold, whose courage to grow with me in love and intimacy is unbounded.

Foreword

We live in an era of impatience. We have learned to throw in the towel when times are tough and the road ahead is dark and confused. In many ways it has become easier to get divorced from our partners than to get to the other side of those issues that prevent us from having the relationship we so fervently desire.

As a Rabbi, I find that *"What Happened to The Prince I Married?"* elevates relationships into the realm of the sacred. It speaks to issues of faith in oneself, in one's partner and in the ability of the human heart to love deeply and enduringly.

As a woman, I turned to the book during a time of great turbulence in my own marriage. Though my husband and I sought assistance from wonderful therapists and beloved family and friends, it wasn't working. In fact nothing was working and it looked as if we were going to become another statistic.

In the midst of this crisis, I received the manuscript of the book you have in your hands. I read it voraciously, finding truth after truth in each succeeding paragraph. I recognized truths about human beings, about healing, about the challenge of loving another person and the difficulty of loving oneself. I was able to reframe my crisis into an opportunity to become my best self. Imagine that! In the worst times to become my best and most loving self through the resources I already had within me.

I read every page, I did every exercise and every meditation. I marked the pages I wanted to read again. Even while it was touch and go, I learned to pour love, not anger, into my wounds and his. No matter what the outcome, I would be fine, profoundly fine, because I was *being* my finest. And my finest helped to create a space of healing and loving.

The crisis passed. We made it, happily and in love. We made it in part because this book changed my perspective on what it meant to be married. It helped me to recognize the prince I had married and embrace the challenges in our lives with love.

What Happened to the Prince I Married? teaches how to stay together. It teaches about self-respect and tolerance. It teaches how to make our choice of a life partner the right choice, through patience, understanding and, most of all, through love — a love that is nurturing, nourishing, strong and forgiving. A love that knows its boundaries but is elastic enough to stretch. A love that heals.

This book acts as a mirror to our souls by enabling us to reveal our hurts and invoke our healing powers. It can help us acquire the skills to create enduring, loving, committed, intimate and deeply satisfying relationships. Dr. Vettese makes the journey gentle, comforting and exciting.

This is a book to read in times of crises. It provides insights that can make crises more bearable and profoundly increase the possibility of getting what we want from the most trying of life's circumstances. It is also a book to read in good times. For those of us with strong and healthy relationships, it can reveal opportunities for deeper intimacy and knowledge about ourselves and our partners.

Dr. Vettese marries the best of psychological principles, spirituality and women's wisdom to reach deeply into the heart, mind and soul of her reader. She herself beautifully and meaningfully provides a model for intimacy. By sharing so much of her own story, along with vignettes from the lives of others, she helps us find ourselves and the courage to embrace change.

I am sure that you will be as grateful to her as I am, for her wisdom and love, as you reach for greater intimacy in your life.

Rabbi Laurie Coskey
May, 1998

Acknowledgments

I am deeply grateful to my family: Harold, Damien, Michael and Shazara. You have given me the love, support and encouragement I needed to write this book. You have all shared in my process and I thank you from the depths of my soul.

Thank you to Maharishi Mahesh Yogi. Thanks to Marianne Williamson, Terri Akin, Kelly Acosta, Truen Bergen, Deborah Capers, Joy Chu, Bobby Colomby and Donna Abbott, Barbara Comstock, Laurie Coskey and Mark Lohkemper, Rita and Deepak Chopra, Karen Druck, Ken Druck, Donna and Mike Fletcher, Eddie Haisha, Raz and Liza Ingrassi, Lyn and Norman Lear, Mike and Jackie Love, MaryEllen McCabe, Susanna Palomares and Dave Cowan, Scarlet Rivera and Tommy Eyre, Dan and Dana McMannus, Laura and Vince Regalbuto, Ayman and Rowan Sawaf and Julia Simon. Special thanks to Lazaris for the creative psychological tools and deep healing you have provided for me. Deepest appreciation and gratitude to Robert Cooper for your wonderful ideas, contributions and ongoing support. And to my sisters, Serena, Neta and Nora — for years of encouragement, I will be forever grateful. Thanks to my parents, Dorothy and Lou Vettese and Fridl Bloomfield. My heart is filled with love for you.

To those who make my life easier — Diane Roberts, Crystal Hammad, Theresa and Fransisca Alto and Chuck McCaull. I thank you so very much for all you do.

Lastly, words cannot describe my gratitude to my editor and friend, Dianne Schilling. Your support, patience, guidance and belief in my work, as well as your insights and creative input, helped make this a better book. I am so thankful to have you in my life.

Aslan Publishing — Our Mission

Aslan Publishing offers readers a window to the soul via well-crafted and practical self-help books, inspirational books and modern day parables. Our mission is to publish books that uplift the mind, body and spirit.

Living one's spirituality in business, relationships and personal growth is the underlying purpose of our publishing company, and the meaning behind our name, Aslan Publishing. We see the word "Aslan" as a metaphor for living spiritually in the physical world.

Aslan means "lion" in several Middle Eastern languages. The most famous "Aslan" is a lion in *The Chronicles of Narnia* by C.S. Lewis. In these stories, Aslan is the Messiah, the One who appears at critical points in the story in order to point human beings in the right direction. Aslan doesn't preach, he acts. His actions are an inherent expression of who he is.

We hope to point individuals toward joyful, satisfying and healthy relationships with oneself and with others. Our goal is to make a real difference in the everyday lives of our readers.

— Barbara & Harold Levine, Publishers

Aslan
PUBLISHING

Contents

Exercises

Introduction

I don't know what to do about my husband's argumentative nature. We never have a beginning, middle and end to our conversations because he constantly interrupts me and becomes defensive. He says that it's my responsibility to change.

~

My husband has become detached and sealed off from me. When I break down in front of him in frustration, he doesn't respond. We have no passion together — he's so cold and unavailable. Since this is his second marriage, you'd think he'd try harder.

~

I feel as though my partner controls me emotionally. He uses money as a weapon in our marriage. If I adhere to his demands and

1

do what he says, he takes me on a trip or buys me something I want.
I don't feel at all safe. I'm afraid of doing or saying the wrong thing,
because I know he'll get upset with me. I feel lost inside. The passion
isn't there and the emotional tension between us is affecting our two
children.

Sound familiar? These are the words of three very different, very real and very frustrated women. They probably represent more women than you or I would believe. In fact, millions of women struggle to understand their difficult mates and the beast that lies within their thwarted relationships. Whether he wears an angry, controlling, jealous, cruel, or simply indifferent face, the beast within the male heart is very real. At their core, many men are deeply wounded.

These wounds may have no obvious outward symptoms. While a man may at times be caring, fun, hardworking, loving and open — the unaware and unhealthy beast that lives beneath this exterior undermines whatever good he demonstrates. He may be unable to feel deep emotions, thus making intimacy virtually nonexistent.

He may be a master at hiding his wounds and may even take pride in his ability to look perfect. Every issue that erupts is the woman's problem, the woman's fault. The "right time" for a sit-down dialogue never seems to present itself. He is too busy, too stressed and overworked. Some women feel continually terrorized by professional and educated husbands. I often hear comments such as, "I don't think things will ever change. Men just aren't capable of giving emotionally."

Some women feel they are engaged in a subtle torture that confines and restricts their ability to love. They ache inside for change, but don't know how to achieve it. Women who have learned to ignore their heartache underestimate how much their pain and resentment cripple them. Many become afraid, blistered, enraged or confused. They want out of their relationships, but are paralyzed by dependence and responsibilities to children.

Many of the women who come to me for therapy are unaware of how much of their self they've lost in their relationship. They may be aware of the toxic energy and emotional turmoil between themselves and their mate, but have no ability to pull out of it. Their survival mechanism is denial steeped in ambivalence. They know no other way to live. Countless times, my role has been to give women a sense of their rights as individuals and to show them there is another way to live, beyond their suffering.

A woman in a difficult relationship often feels as if she were living with a beast, not a man. What she doesn't realize is that her mate's terrible disposition calls forth another beast — the one in her. Whether bitter, controlling, paranoid, righteous, blaming, denying, fearful, frustrated, envious or gushingly compliant, every woman in an unfulfilling relationship has undesirable and unhealthy qualities — the outward manifestations of *her* beast. The beast can become a highly useful and constructive part of a woman's personality, but only if she faces and learns to control its most destructive qualities.

A woman is conditioned to ignore her inner beast. She denies her rage, fury, and dark energy, robbing herself of the power she needs to engage comfortably in male-female interactions. This potent beast can become a powerful guide, helping her to change the negative visage of her relationship. By learning to rely on this fierce power, she can redirect her love and passion into areas that fulfill her while releasing the hurt, anger, shame and guilt that may currently surround her heart.

We attract into our lives the level of woundedness in a man that we have within ourselves. Many women find it difficult to relate to this concept. Some have been raised in homes where the male figure, the father, was respectful, kind, nurturing, responsible and shared equally in the care of the family unit.

Others recall nothing in their childhood that foreshadowed the turmoil they experience with their partners. Some have a deep desire for fantasy, and attract adventurous, uncommitted and more worldly men, then live through these men until they wake up to their unhappiness. Regardless of individual motivation, the women I counsel almost always discover the details and intricacies of their woundedness through their relationships.

Our complex internal struggles, our suffering, anger, hurt, repression, confusion and pain are not just a result of what men do to us, but more importantly of what we do to ourselves in reaction to their behavior. Women are not necessarily healthier than men. Many women are addicted to pain and have such fears of being left or abandoned that they allow behaviors which should not be tolerated. Women cause just as much pathology in relationships as men by claiming they are victims and continuing to live as victims in a partnership of marriage.

To change her relationship, however, a woman needs more than the positive qualities of her inner beast; she must nourish and exercise the primordial wisdom of the caring heart. She needs specific knowledge and information about how to bring about change, which requires understanding certain psychological dynamics of the male ego: why men resist their feelings, why they hurt, why they are afraid to grow, and how to help them accept deep emotion. In addition, a woman needs guidance in applying her knowledge to specific destructive behavior patterns within the relationship itself. When she is challenged by her partner's beast, she must see through the eyes of her own beast and use this knowledge and passion to courageously challenge the situation. She must set healing boundaries and stand up to him in a new way.

This book speaks to those of you who are struggling to love a wounded and difficult man, and who have the courage to face the truth of your total life. If you commit to healing *your* woundedness, positive changes are inevitable. The key is to recognize that your man is often raging outside because he is so deeply wounded inside, and to identify where both of you are hurting so that you can effect change — first within yourself, then within your mate.

By recognizing his anger, vulnerability, and deep hurt and using his actions as a catalyst for change, you can untie the knots that you and you alone secured. You are the one who brought him in. Now use his presence in your life as a point of reference to help steer you to deeper levels of healing. A sacred bond has developed between you and your lover that has shape, meaning and purpose. Chaos and order work together. Be willing to understand the meaning they have in your life with your man.

You cannot fix a man who chooses to be abusive. That is not your responsibility. On the other hand, it *is* your responsibility to retrieve hope and reclaim your life. When you take steps toward this goal, your partner is likely to show increased signs of respect. However, if he continues to mistreat you, and you are unwilling to leave the abusive situation, you must seriously confront your own lack of self-worth.

What Happened to the Prince I Married is filled with basic yet profound truths that will gently and lovingly encourage you to explore the truth of your relationship. If you are ready, this book will help you:

• Dive heart first into the beast. Turn your most destructive self into a constructive and positive force that powerfully heals your wounded relationship. When you accept your beastly nature, you will find the beauty — the love — that lies within. The essence of your power exists not in your outer shell, but in your soul, where the beast and beauty merge. This book will help you learn to express your beast in communication with your partner, safely showing him your strength.

• Realize that his wounding is your growth edge, and that you can heal him through your willingness to heal yourself. You are already aware of this intuitively. Now you need the steps. When you are exquisitely tuned-in to the needs of your mate and yourself, you will instinctively know what actions to take to effect change. By allowing his wounding to be your growth edge, you can use your difficult mate's characteristics as a catalyst for change.

• Establish secure emotional boundaries that shield your heart from the insensitive behavior of your wounded man. You have the ability to render harmless all the hurtful comments and immature actions that he uses to belittle, subdue or control you. Learn to turn his emotional outbursts into windows through which you see into his wounded core, rather than spears that penetrate your caring heart.

• Recognize your spiritual esteem as the entire essence of your being, and the most powerful contributing factor to the emotional health of your relationship. Self-esteem is something you must earn. Spiritual esteem is something you already possess! This book shows you how to find it, trust it, and use its healing energy.

• Use the hidden power of the loving heart to end martyrdom and self-deprecating behavior. This is the only power that can tame the beast within your mate. Invoke your healing powers to remove the cover from your mate's sealed heart, using your own life as an instrument. Every negative quality in him relates to an unhealthy part of you. Using this perspective to draw him into your heart, you will achieve a deep and intimate love.

1

When You Love a Wounded Man

*The task is to go as deeply as possible into the darkness,
to name the pain that one finds there, and the truth of one's
perceptions, and to emerge on the other side.*
— Anthea Francine
Envisioning Theology

He is impenetrable and closed, insensitive to the emotional needs around him.   He fears being vulnerable, often appearing shut down or stone-faced while you bare to him your most heartfelt feelings. He is afraid of his own neediness and often hides that neediness under a "cool" or disinterested facade. He is haunted by inner struggles that you can do little about.

He may be self-indulgent and narcissistic, unaware of how self-possessed he is. Though he occasionally expresses a desire for intimacy, in actuality he is unable to reveal deeper feelings about his life — particularly painful feelings. He probably doesn't know the pain is there.   Or he may be vaguely aware of an ache that has no recognizable form or definition.

When he is struggling internally, he often creates external conflict (usually with you) to avoid facing what is really going on. He is easily distracted by "more important" stuff in his life, like work, projects, and outside interests, which leaves you feeling rejected and unimportant.

The man I'm describing might have one of these characteristics or many, but one thing is certain — you live with him. And although he is the man you love, he can be degrading, disengaged, possessive, critical, hurtful, and hard to approach.

You may find yourself walking a fine line, trying to stay balanced between the polarities of his personality. Your heart's wishes for healing and openness seem futile while you are stuck with him in a survival mode. The two of you can be together one moment and disconnected the next — a single incident causing the flow of love to be interrupted. The climb back into the heart space may seem impossible or, at the very least, excruciatingly difficult.

You are secretly aware that his feelings of rage and love overwhelm him at times, but his pain goes unacknowledged and unexpressed. He survives and copes, but he doesn't connect.

Despite all this, he has a side that you love — one that is somehow familiar to you. Parts of his personality — the parts you fell in love with — are endearing to you. You know he is perfect on one level, yet struggle intensely to understand how to respond to his unhealthy and immature side. Your attempts to intervene, or just to understand, are met with defensiveness. Your efforts to achieve connectedness are either misunderstood or viewed with suspicion.

A woman who has learned to ignore her own heartache underestimates how much she is crippled by the pain and resentment that build inside her. Afraid, blistered, enraged, or confused, she may want out of the relationship, but be paralyzed by her own overwhelming guilt and low self-esteem. A woman in a difficult relationship often feels terrorized, as if she is living with a beast, not a man.

Beauty and the Beast

Who is this male beast and how has he come to be with you? Only you can answer these questions.

Initially, you draw the beast to you out of love. By seeking to truly understand him and what he has to teach you, you discover much about yourself. This powerful force, the beast in him, needs to be accepted. By accepting him you accept the deepest levels of your own experience and begin to integrate elements of your own beast. Yes, dear reader, there are really two beasts in this picture — his and yours — and they are related. Like brother and sister, they share a common gene.

The female beast has permission to emerge when faced with the male beast. Looking at the classic fairy tale, we get a clear picture of how this works:

In *Beauty and the Beast,* a beggar woman seeks shelter at the castle of a handsome prince, offering a single rose as payment. Infuriated by the demand that he open his home — and heart — the prince refuses. In turning away from the beggar woman, the prince scorns love and compassion, shuns the light, embraces darkness and turns into an ugly Beast — the physical embodiment of his own cruelty and selfishness. Only love can break the spell.

Living with her father in a nearby village is Belle, a loyal, loving daughter who rebuffs her pompous suitor, Gaston, and dreams of adventure. Belle represents those of us who want more than a provincial life.

Traveling through the woods, Belle's father becomes lost, stumbles upon the enchanted castle and is taken prisoner by the Beast. Belle finds her father in the castle and begs for his release. The Beast makes an offer — the old man in exchange for Belle. Out of love for her father, Belle stays. Over time, Belle's compassion, firmness, and loving tutelage gently ply and then powerfully penetrate the armor of the Beast, and he begins to change.

A series of interventions by Belle's father and Gaston slow but fail to halt love's conquering destiny. In conversations, walks, touches, and play, Belle's caring reaches beyond the Beast's coarse, defensive surface and touches his sad and wounded core. In love, the spell is shattered and the Prince emerges, reborn.

Many of us have encountered a defensive partner — a beast — when we have sought to make a heart-to-heart connection. Somehow this request for intimacy feels like a threat to the man, who moves to protect and preserve his masculine nature.

Your disappointments and confrontations feed his low self-image, just like Belle's fed those of the cursed prince. The beast quietly shames himself for failing at love. He is suspicious and mistrusting of your wish to deepen the language of the heart.

This continued rejection leads to despair and then deep woundedness. His wounding becomes your wounding. In time, your love is so weathered that anger is your only companion and a sealed heart your means to survive. If left unattended, this anger is a poisonous brew that deadens all possibility of healing and love. It must be understood and embraced. Your most important lessons exist in the depths of your anger and rage — where *your* beast lives.

The reason you are not attracted to the safe, committed, mature man is that he has nothing to teach you. Gaston, in *Beauty and the Beast,* is the perfect reminder of this. Although he exudes abundant clues to the superficiality of his existence, he would certainly be a more comfortable choice for Belle. Something in her pushes him away. She wants to know more about herself, and will risk lessons of the heart elsewhere.

Belle leaves her nest to look for her father who is lost in the woods, following her instincts until she comes upon him in the Prince's castle. Similarly, you and I have left familiar and comfortable places to reach deeper into our relationship with the "father" figure, to know more about the love and confusion that we feel in the most private recesses of our psyche.

Out of Belle's love for her father, she stays with the Beast. What a perfect metaphor for growth! Belle embraces the darkness and the demon, trusting that change will occur. She reminds us to use our fierceness and face the beastly side of our mate, even if we are afraid that he will consume or control us. Like Belle, we often retreat into ourselves because we have been overpowered. Yet, we must have courage and patience, trusting that one day our desires will be met.

The rose symbolizes the heart of the Beast. When Belle gets close to his heart, the Beast rages. He yells at her to get out. She runs away as fast as she can. Too often, we have exposed our partner's heart and are met with anger. Such direct attacks cause us to want to run away. We find the man repulsive in these moments, so we often leave emotionally, the pain of rejection overwhelming our courage.

The wolves that Belle meets in the woods are her own inner struggles — the aggressive and frightening echoes of her consciousness. They must be loud enough to capture Belle's attention or she will ignore them. You have these reminders in your dreams or through the voices of your own inner wolves. Similarly, when the Beast picks up the wolf, he demonstrates his willingness to struggle with the dark and raging force within himself.

The real breakthrough occurs at the point where Belle's fury and passion meet the Beast's fury and passion. Belle is able to harness her aggression and use it to do what she must to get what she wants.

You have probably felt a similar kind of aggression at times when face to face with the beast in your partner. Your instinctual thirst for truth leads you into this potent energy. Trusting how that energy is meant to be used causes your own beast to emerge.

These are electric moments in time — moments when you are ignited by the passion of the beast. You feel drawn to know this male force in the most intimate possible way. A part of you is terrified by his darkness, but in a strange way that dark force is familiar. Your heart has met its supreme challenge. If you want to know yourself, stay and learn. If you want to know the power in your heart, the shadow of the beast will guide you.

In the fairy tale, the Beast continues to use his power through negative means, and is confronted with a gentle, caring heart far more powerful in love than he is in rage. Belle brings him to this place of knowing through her wisdom, self-assurance, and inner strength. Belle feels secure within herself even when his pain is overwhelming. He is exposed and vulnerable. He confronts his wounded core in the presence of a safe and trusting love.

In those rare moments when your mate lets you glimpse his true nature — vulnerable, loving, tender — you sense that you have found an opening into his heart. It is in these moments that your own healing and growth in love occur. To know him truly — without judgment — you must allow him to expose his wounds to you. He will never trust you if you are unwilling to look deeply into the part of his heart where rage and confusion live, where his mind aches. Here you will learn your own lessons, too. You will experience insights that relate to unfinished business from your own past. Everything he presents to you will correspond with necessary increments in your own growth. The more you embrace these dark and frightening images, the more power you will have in all areas of your life.

The Beast learns how to be a friend and have fun. Belle learns to trust her heart through the Beast's eyes, especially where her father is concerned. When he holds up the mirror, she feels the pain instantly. She knows she must deal with her own lessons and takes the mirror with her as a reminder to do this.

The real breakthrough for Belle occurs when she confronts Gaston. She establishes boundaries and stands up to him force-fully, defying his control over her. She defines her position through self-love, determination, and will.

Without firm and loving boundaries, you and I will never fully love and be loved in the way that we desire and deserve. The boundaries you attempt to set in relationship with your mate will rarely be met with detachment. Change doesn't happen instantly. Allow the negative consequences that you experience each time you take a stand to serve as catalysts, helping you get from one place to the next. If you are afraid of the consequences, you will never know who you really are. The next time you stand up for yourself or set a boundary, the negative reaction will be less intense than the one before, and so on.

Men are not accustomed to relating in this way. They must change and learn to honor the feminine. In the end, the old must die off, making way for the new.

Gaston and the Beast surrender to the wisdom of the feminine, becoming as if one in the heart. No longer is there a need to go to battle because the payoff, through the heart, is far more satisfying than the fight for power. When you and your lover are able to look deeply into each other's soul and embrace all that you see, beauty finds the beast and the beast finds beauty. Love and passion merge.

The Choice Is Yours

Men are transformed by their pain into the insensitive beasts that break women's hearts. The irony is that the power to change the relationship lies within the woman's heart — your heart. Power comes from discovering your deep inner beauty and inner beast, from embracing your own wounding, from exploiting the power of your caring heart. You are longing to know the transforming power that lies within you. You are curious to know what dark, negative force is being mirrored to you from the depths of your struggle with your mate.

At its core all wounding is intricate, detailed, and chaotic. When you love a wounded man you thirst for understanding and healing, yet the struggle drains you of energy. You are aware of the wild beast that appears to be tangled in his own web of woundedness. Your freedom will come as you explore why you have chosen this life mate, this life script. The reasons are deep, rich, and beautifying to your soul.

Duality lives in every one of us — it is a force that rages, fights, destroys, and conquers. Yet it also heals, supports, nurtures, and protects. All life is the integration of two polarities of energy. For any relationship to reach its full potential, the male and female beasts must merge.

The greatest lesson that *Beauty and the Beast* offers us is that a thing must be loved before it is lovable. The beast that exists in our lives must be understood, felt, and seen. It must stand before us like a giant force with all of its fury and power.

Your greatest learning lies in knowing who the male beast is, and how and why he has come to be with you.

Your partner appeared at first to be a prince. For mysterious reasons, he touched something deep inside of you, satisfying a need or fulfilling a deep desire. Perhaps there was an element of danger to the relationship that fed your longings. Though impractical, you wanted it. What you didn't realize was how much you were setting up this prince to disappoint you. You fell deeply in love and were optimistic about the relationship, but ignored inner messages of the work ahead of you.

Setting out unconsciously to experience adventure and excitement, you ended up in a wounded relationship. You attracted the very thing that now repels you. Why? Because that is where your greatest learning awaits — where the journey is exhilarating beyond your wildest dreams.

It is in the depths of your darkest feelings that you can change your story of love. Here you are free to release the past and reinvent the future. You can learn to:

1. Allow his wounding to be your growth edge, your catalyst for change.
2. Identify his wounding and your wounding.
3. Find hidden power through love rather than despair.
4. Use your passionate beast to create deep intimate conversation.
5. Understand why spiritual esteem is a step beyond self-esteem.
6. Regain your creative energy and use it to heal others.
7. Reach a new level of commitment to your own growth.
8. Find the inspiration and inner power to rewrite your story of love.

Your Wounding As a Catalyst

Your true identity is hidden in your own wounding. Your broken relationships hold all the clues to how you can heal old hurts and move on to release for all time the negative patterns of the past.

I am often confronted with weeds in my garden, amidst all of the beautiful flowers. If I were to ignore the weeds and fail to pluck them, then all the color, fragrance, and beauty of the flowers would be overrun with a powerful destructive force that would twist itself around the beauty and engulf it.

Your own wounding is like a garden full of weeds. You must go into your garden with your sleeves rolled up, ready to face whatever you find. Begin by observing carefully, noticing the rhythms of your garden and identifying one by one the destructive forces that live there. Be willing to pluck out each weed and examine its relationship to the rest of the garden. How did it get there? Who brought it in? Why is it there? What are you meant to learn from its presence? Through this effort you will regain control of this beautiful space. Just as your wounding is painful and dark, your willingness to go into the dirt that holds your garden's life force will unveil secrets about you and new pathways to beauty. You will smell the sweetness of new life that flourishes in a well-tended garden.

My Wounding

At the age of ten, I knew that my father was unfaithful to my mother. He would stay out for one or two nights in a row and my mother would become depressed. She would seal herself over emotionally to cope with the pain of rejection. She was exhausted all the time, slept long hours and tried her best to keep the busy household functioning. When he did come home, he would bring presents to try to alleviate his guilt. I was very aware of their troubled marriage and angry with both of them for the confusion in our household. We were seven out-of-control children with two depressed, angry parents.

This is when the beast in me was fueled. To survive the daily struggles that went on between brothers and sisters who were always fighting and raging, I became the caretaker. I had to do something, so trying to create order out of chaos by cleaning up the continually messy kitchen and helping my mother cook became a daily ritual and an outlet.

I left home at fifteen, love-starved and pregnant, making a pact with myself never to repeat the destructive life I'd had as a child. After going through the heartache of giving up my child for adoption, creating a life for myself was no easy task.

At eighteen, I married a man who seemed to be the opposite of my father. I felt relieved to be free of my dysfunctional past and to share my life with this new person. Unfortunately, I had no idea how to have a lasting and intimate relationship. I was terrified of confrontation, having witnessed my mother's emotional and sometimes physical abuse, and soon began to rage inside at conditions in my marriage that troubled me. My husband had his own way of coping. He detached himself from our life by leaving home for months at a time — work took him away. We lived separate lives during our entire ten-year marriage with nothing but our two children holding us together. How ironic it was: In essence I had recreated my mother's life. My husband and I spent no time in shared communication and neither of us realized we had a living, useful beast inside that could have helped heal our old wounds and renew our love. The beast in each of us lay dormant.

When I found out that my husband had fallen in love with a woman he'd been seeing for the last three years of our marriage, I was completely torn apart. I knew about the relationship long before our separation, but sealed over my anger and confusion because I was too afraid to deal with it. When I finally embraced the truth, I felt devastated. It was what I had grown up with. My father continually had affairs with other women, and I swore I would never allow myself to be similarly deceived.

Even before I had formally ended my marriage and dealt with all of my dark feelings of pain and rage, I was falling in love with another man who loved women and prided himself on being free. His attitude of "make love, not war" seemed reasonable to me, but somewhere deep inside I felt a gnawing ache. My denial was so great that I was attracted to the very thing that promised to cause me the most grief. My attraction to him completely clouded the reality I had lived with since I was a little girl.

Once again I had chosen a man who, on the surface, looked very different from my father. Like a fairy-tale prince, he rescued me from an unhappy life. I didn't realize how unloved and miserable I felt until I met him. He opened up a whole new world — a world I had never known. When he beckoned, an unknown part of me emerged — a different woman came forward. It was as though an ache, or longing, was being satisfied. He was enthralled with me, believed in my abilities, listened to me, and offered ideas about a new way of living. He was magical and very loving. His attentions drew me in.

What I completely denied was that the basis on which our relationship was formed lacked commitment and practicality. This man wanted to remain free to love other women. He was unable to make a commitment to marriage. He wavered back and forth, talking about his fear of marriage, but I knew that the real issue was his inability to experience true intimacy with just one person. He had enjoyed superficial relationships with different women for many years. That was comfortable for him.

The honesty was painful. He wasn't ready to settle down. I was. In my mind, I said wishfully, "Sometime soon, he will come to his senses and realize that I am enough for him." I didn't want to give up all the other things I had with him, so I felt I had to change him. To experience the excitement of my new relationship, I was willing to ignore the pain deep in my heart, and the knowledge that an open relationship was not what I wanted.

My Awakening

Eventually this man "gave in" to my desire for a monogamous relationship and we were married. Today we have a healthy, strong and lasting love relationship, but it did not come easily. I want to share with you each step of my growth and healing process, in the hope that understanding what I went through will help you to heal your wounds of love and find the beauty in your partner — and the beast in you.

Years after we were married, my husband confessed an eighteen-month-long fling. I was furious and heartbroken. How could this happen to me again? I was crushed at my core — broken apart in a million pieces. He was sorry and remorseful; he even asked for my forgiveness.

Shock gave way to depression, and I didn't know what to do. So I continued my very demanding schedule, seeing clients, keeping our family together, and overseeing the household. In an effort to burn off my fury, I went to the gym. One night after a particularly heavy workout, I came home exhausted. I was alone in the house, since my husband was away on business. I had a light supper and went to bed early. I had been aware all day of an aching deep in my chest, an emptiness and pain that would not go away. I longed for sleep and relief.

Lying in bed, I began to look within. I had never felt so alone. I reflected on my life, asking myself, "How could this be happening to me again?" I had confronted this issue and worked on it at length. I understood that I was attracted to the kind of man who looked to other women for fulfillment. My father was unfaithful to my mother. My ex-husband was unfaithful to me. I believed that I had finally ended the issue of infidelity. I was mistaken.

It had taken me years to trust my husband, and now that trust was gone. I felt horribly wounded. The pain of what I had done to myself overwhelmed me. The weight of sorrow was so heavy that all I could do was lie down on my bed. My world had fallen apart. I felt alienated. Despite the fact that we were both therapists, knowledgeable in the tools of reconciliation, my husband and I were rapidly growing apart.

My ideas of marriage as a voyage haunted me. Standing on the bridge, watching my whole life head for the rocks, no amount of self-talk could help me. I felt alone and completely helpless. My children and I had already suffered the terrible anguish of one divorce. Now I was watching history repeat itself, with enormous pain in store for everyone closest to me. My despair grew as I lay there in the dark. The weight of pain on my chest pulled me deeper and deeper into despair. I experienced a force drawing me into the darkness within my soul. All I could imagine was that my heart was finally breaking as I acknowledged truths about myself and my life. But none of my rationalizations, expectations or admissions seemed to lessen the pain. Drowning in my own anguish, I finally decided to just let go and immerse myself in the sorrow and darkness of my soul.

Tears streamed down the side of my face onto the pillow as I lay in silence feeling the enormous depth of my anger and pain. My mind kept trying to figure out why I was hurting so much. Why? Why? But intuitively I recognized these questions as my mind's effort to rationalize the pain rather than embrace the truth. Instead of blaming anyone else for my pain, I decided to do something I had never done before. One by one, as each new sad, angry or painful thought emerged, I let it wash over me and then propelled it through a tunnel of love that led from the center of my heart all the way out into the vast universe of light and eternity.

Through this process, I encountered a dimension of love that I have since recognized as my connection to an eternal feminine heart. This heart holds all the universe within it. It is a love so great and safe that not even death can change its impact.

This encounter came quite unexpectedly. Watching my negative and despairing thoughts traverse this tunnel brought relief so welcome in the midst of my despair that I continued the process. Soon, I noticed a sense of inner lightness unfolding as each turbulent thought disappeared into eternity. At some point I felt completely transparent. My body disappeared and I found myself basking in a vast field of light and joy that I had never known before. My heart felt like it had expanded to the limits of the universe. I felt my whole body suffused and ignited by love flowing through me and from me with no limit or restriction. A profound transformation had originated at the very core of my psyche.

When I finally opened my eyes, I did not realize how long I had been lying on my bed. What was immediately clear was that I had changed. In place of my despair and emptiness, I now found a quiet joy and transparent fullness. I felt connected, grounded, impassioned, and alive again. The weight was gone. Replacing the grief and despair was ecstasy — a kind I had never known.

While the overwhelming immediacy of this experience has faded with time, its significance has not only remained but grown. What I realize is that I accessed the dimension of my psyche that mystics, theologians and psychologists have long identified as the primordial feminine soul. I also learned that I could draw on this inner resource of energy, peace, and wisdom in a simple way, as a peasant woman draws water from a well.

The tapline to this fountainhead of inner strength was the tender impulse of caring. My own aching and willingness to surrender to my pain took me there. The same qualities of the caring heart that were the source of so much pain were also the source of enormous power. What I had lost — self-respect and self-esteem — were given back to me through my willingness to receive. In this experience of spiritual esteem, I recognized that I needed to focus all of my power on my ideals and on the choices that served me and my children. I realized that I never had, and never would have, control over what my partner did, but that I did possess the power to further my own growth and thereby be a catalyst in his growth. This experience may have been the very thing that began an intense healing process for both of us.

Deeper Resolution

A few days later, I decided to revisit the deep, loving peace I had experienced that night, to see what would emerge when I felt whole.

Recalling the joy and light I experienced deep within my being, I took myself back into that love by closing my eyes and remembering its beauty. At the center of the light, I saw my mother dealing with exactly the same issue — the issue of infidelity — and her mother, and her mother's mother. I could see all the way back through time. This had been in my family for generations, and I had been carrying its accumulated weight. Realizing the impact that this remarkable situation had on me, I felt free to give back the weight and pain I had carried for my mother and grandmother — indeed, for a long procession of ancestral women — owning only that which was mine.

Understanding how and why I had attracted these conditions in the first place represented an amazing breakthrough for me. I felt completely released from their weight and sorrow for all time. I no longer needed such conditions in my life. I felt as if my blueprint had changed. This dramatic shift enabled me to begin to openly communicate my thoughts and deeper feelings to my husband with neither a hidden agenda nor any great fear of the consequences. We began to talk about the deeper meaning of my experience, and he understood the intimate feelings I had about my own process.

My vulnerability and openness led him to look more deeply into his own wounding. While part of me longed for him to know the origins of his pain, I knew I had to be patient, and continually reminded myself that he was on his time frame, not mine.

Eventually, my husband realized that he had felt confined within a controlling feminine force ever since he was a little boy. This conflict, and the deeper pain of seeing his parents miserably trapped in a hostile marriage within suffocatingly close quarters, had persuaded him to avoid intimacy and stop feeling altogether. He had decided, "If I can't feel, I can't be hurt."

This is what my husband had projected onto me, but in reality it had little to do with me. The irony is that my father had avoided intimacy and feelings in the same way my husband did. My husband was raging inside, still behaving like an angry adolescent, one who had been mortally wounded as a child. This was his beast! I remember wondering to, myself, "Why is it that he seems so out of touch with what I'm feeling about his infidelity?" In truth, he *was* out of touch! He could not let my feelings in, because he would feel guilty, and he hated his mother for manipulating him with guilt. He was angry, confused and deeply hurt over things that happened to him as a child. How could he possibly have compassion for me when he had none for himself? A man cannot give what he doesn't have. He was bankrupt. I was his mirror playing the role of mother in his life. He was my mirror playing the role of father in my life.

Being vulnerable felt new and different for him. But the knowledge that he wanted our love to expand and mature kept me in the relationship. As long as he wished to grow as much as I did, and was willing to stay on the path of learning, I felt rewarded.

Confronting with Passion

Finally, I decided that I was ready to get in the ring with him once and for all — to have it out about his infidelity. I knew his behavior was a result of his immaturity and that he loved me deeply, but I also knew that his transgressions hurt me and undermined our growth as individuals and as a couple. I refused to continue in a marriage that did not embody the highest values of mutual respect and trust. Because infidelity was such a big issue at my core, I realized that I had to raise my expectations.

I deserved more. It had taken me a long time to feel my worth and to know fully that I had changed. At last I was ready to be treated with the utmost respect and equality. It was important to put the issue of infidelity behind me.

I decided to attempt a breakthrough in our relationship. I didn't want to threaten him with divorce or berate him with accusations. What I wanted was for us to achieve a new depth in relating to each other. I wanted to know that he fully understood and experienced the pain that he had caused me. Further, I wanted to know that, out of love for me, he would choose to control his impulses and show respect for our marriage.

Going into this effort, I knew it would be difficult and I was ready. Healing my wounds and having an experience of the beast in me helped prepare me to heal my relationship. No matter how effective my husband was at his work, he was also a typical male. He was reticent to acknowledge his own pain and resistant to acknowledging mine. Empathy with others was much easier than empathy with one's wife — the intense feelings cut too close to home.

Prior to the crucial heart session with my husband, I planned very carefully. To lessen the likelihood of his immediate rejection, I let time be my friend. I was cognizant that my goal was mutual growth, not merely expression of my hurt or manipulation of his behavior.

When we finally sat down together, I thought of myself as a boxer ready to go a long fifteen rounds. But I also kept my objective in mind. I wasn't trying to knock him down, but rather to open him up. So I began to talk about his infidelity and to acknowledge him for his confession and apology. I also explained that this wasn't enough. There was something more that I needed from him to heal the hurt that lay deep within my heart. As I had anticipated, he became defensive, and we got into a long discussion about why women keep recalling past hurts with the men in their lives.

When I mentioned the affairs that had occurred earlier in our marriage, my husband accused me of once again dragging up the ancient past. Rather than respond angrily to his demeaning attitude, I chose to come from my heart. I explained that the reason women frequently refer to past hurts is that men don't fully acknowledge their woman's pain. Men are not required to agree with everything that a woman shares. Simply standing open-hearted, listening and receiving the information will create a beginning, middle and end to the communication. In her mind, the issue will shift from loud angry noise to background information. She will have much more to give, in love, once this happens.

I began to sob, revealing all of my anguish, taking the risk of complete self-disclosure. The waves of my pain were too much for my husband's defenses. His heart began to open with the realization that I had been deeply wounded by his playful escapades. At that moment, while revealing my recent pain, the little girl inside me was overcome by the grief she had witnessed as a child. I realized the degree to which I had taken on my mother's deep anguish about my father's infidelity, and in my mind's eye I could see my grandmother's and great-grandmother's sorrow at having to deal with this same issue. I felt a sense of relief, as if the wound inside me had completely opened up and all the diseased emotional matter had flowed out, leaving me empty and open. My psychic wall came tumbling down, and years of holding back in mistrust disappeared. I felt my heart open and I knew that healing had begun. My willingness to be deeply vulnerable created a bridge for renewal that allowed us to go forward. In loving myself so fully, I loved my husband. We knew things would be different between us after that.

Later, looking back on this effort, I realized that I had created powerful change. I had achieved what I needed at the moment — understanding and respect. I also realized that I still had a great deal of work to do, both within myself and for my marriage. But this was an important step. I knew that to completely resolve this painful issue, I had to stay in my marriage and be one-hundred percent committed to completing the legacy. I also realized how effective I had been at bringing down my husband's defenses. I made it safe for love to deepen, first within myself and then in our relationship.

My husband and I continue our growth as individuals and as a couple, and I truly believe that the healthy, honest and rewarding love relationship we enjoy today is due largely to a willingness on the part of both of us to allow this painful and difficult process to facilitate our individual growth. By going all the way to the bottom of our feelings — to the darkest place — we have healed our childhood wounds.

I now recognize it was my destiny to deal with these love and intimacy issues. I acknowledge that these conflicts, somehow written into my life script, presented many opportunities for spiritual growth! I dove into the depths of my struggle and pain to rise up overflowing with joy and freedom. I woke up to my worth. My husband was not the culprit, he was a catalyst, enabling me to close the chapter on infidelity.

There are no perfect relationships, no right or wrong answers, simply levels of commitment to growth throughout life.

2

The Beast That Lives in Beauty

Wherever snow falls, or water flows, or birds fly,
wherever day and night meet in twighlight,
wherever the blue heaven is hung by clouds, or sown with stars,
wherever are forms with transparent boundaries,
wherever are outlets into celestial space,
wherever is danger and awe, and love,
there is beauty, plentious as rain, shed for thee.
—Ralph Waldo Emerson

For many of us, one of the most difficult challenges is to look deep within for hidden, unresolved issues. Examine the dramas in your life and you will see exactly where you need to grow and heal. By seeking deeper resolution you will experience a lifting of the spirit — a lightened soul — and enjoy a freer existence.

Many women are unaware of how many layers of troublesome issues and anxieties they carry around in the far corners of their psyches. By opening your heart and soul to deeper meaning in your relationship, you will effortlessly dispel some of these shadows. When you discover in yourself the source of an issue, your capacity to produce miracles in your life will be extraordinary.

A woman's challenge is to find the courage to sustain her own growth while naturally assisting in the growth of her relationship. I know that I have my own issues to focus on. As a result, there will always be depths of intimacy and love unfolding in my relationship. Each time I recognize and invoke the power within my heart to change *me*, approximating more closely the person I want to be, a beautiful shift occurs in my relationship with my husband and in our life together.

While my story may seem dramatic to some, others of you are attempting to manage situations far more painful and challenging than mine. We each have a story that serves as our reference to life.

Only you know the extent of your private pain. Just as I have descended into a dark place, you too are already directed toward this fierce and passionate terrain. The story of love that you have in your life right now is your mirror.

Do not be afraid, but if you are, allow this fear to help you reach places you never before dared go.

Surrender to your difficult issues and give the beast a chance to appear. Unlock the door and open it up, revealing what has been behind it for a very long time. You can begin by trusting what you've been through, giving up the role of victim (silently walking through your days) or martyr (pretending that life is all right) and exposing yourself to the true feelings of the beast inside you.

When your beast has a chance to be seen, your life will change. There is no turning back from this point because it is love — self-love — that encourages the beast to appear, and love always multiplies itself. Every new truth about how your beast fits into your life will help transform the darkness into incomparable beauty.

The beast is a good thing in you. She is your fierceness. The beast is the part of you that is angry, hurt, unhappy, out of control. Her powerful energy directs your attention to areas of your life that must be changed.

The male beast that points the way is less important now. You are passing into the realm of your own greatness.

Preparing for Change

In order to move forward and draw out the beast, we must first know the complexities of our life. Our woman's heart is both a blessing and a curse. The blessing stems from our instinctual caring for others coupled with our natural sensitivity to the rich tapestry of human feelings. Unlike a lot of men, we are not afraid to care about others. Rather, because we care, we are drawn to define ourselves in terms of our relationships. We yearn to have our feelings acknowledged by others just as much as we strive to show others that we understand their feelings.

However, because of our heightened capacity to care, we often feel cursed. We experience the pain of others as our own, and insensitivity to our pain, particularly from the man in our life, registers as a cut at the core of our being. The caring heart bleeds easily and, more often than not, the bleeding remains deeply hidden. Many of us cope with these internal lacerations by growing psychic scar tissue. Those of us who have been wounded over and over again are probably very reluctant to open our caring heart to the same person who wounded us. We feel even greater wariness toward new love.

One woman compared her loss of caring to an experimental process in which the homing behavior in pigeons was extinguished: First the pigeons were conditioned to expect positive reinforcement in the form of food when they reached their destination. They flew faster in anticipation of receiving the food. When the amount of food was decreased, the behavior of the pigeons changed. They no longer flew swiftly. Eventually, when no food awaited them, the pigeons gave up on the destination altogether. This woman described her feelings of caring and love for her partner of thirty years in a similar vein. He was so unable to nourish her caring heart, rejecting her attempts to achieve intimacy, that eventually she stopped wanting to be close. She realized that she could never have what she wanted with him, so she withdrew her love. She built a psychic structure that encapsulated her pain and defended her against future hurt.

Relief for this woman came when she moved from caterpillar — vulnerable and dependent on outside forces for survival — to cocoon. Away from harm's way, in the dark and the pain, she was safe.

Many women become bitter, resentful or fearful, quietly rejecting their mate and at the same time fearing his fury. Instead of unleashing the raging energy they feel, these women become reluctant, tentative and cautious, lost and out of touch with their most valuable asset, the capacity to love. They shut out the nutrients needed to stimulate growth in their hearts. Some work in a crazed frenzy to ward off deep anguish, fearing that if they stop to feel they will fall apart. Others satisfy emotional needs by pouring all the love and energy into their children, which may threaten their mate even more, leading to jealous, needy behavior. These women all live in frustration. Their spirit withers, like a garden gradually cut off from a bubbling spring.

Soul Sisters

To soothe the heartache of living with a difficult male, my mother, my grandmother and, I'm sure, her mother before her all sought comfort from women friends. Though some of us are afraid to confide in our friends, most women instinctively turn to one another for help. Perhaps we talk to each other about our relationships because we recognize the light of a caring heart in our sisters' eyes. Perhaps we talk about our relationships because we empathize with the pain, and we know that talking about the problem helps, although it rarely heals or changes anything in the troubled relationship.

For all the talking we do about our relationships, most of us experience relatively paltry results. We comfort one another, we find solace in hearing that others have the same problems with their husbands or lovers or fathers or brothers. But talking does not heal our deepest wounds or effect real change in our relationships.

I wonder sometimes if there was once an oral tradition of feminine wisdom passed from mother to daughter concerning how to cope with the thorny and often cold male heart. Was this oral tradition lost? Our collective desire to help one another in the struggle to create truly loving relationships is an affirmation that we have more to offer one another, more wisdom in our own hearts, than we may realize or acknowledge. How can we get hold of that wisdom and use it lovingly, through an open, caring heart, with the wounded men in our lives?

While many men have learned to participate and work in the family unit, I am deeply concerned about women who remain victims of a male dominated social order. For all the progress we've made in efforts to gain equality of opportunity and true freedom of choice, reports about the glass ceiling and other limitations on women show that disparities remain.

Less often discussed but equally important is something I see evidence of every day — the dearth of change in the average household. The struggle against male domination at home in all its subtle and not so subtle forms embroils many women in so much anger that they lose touch with their deepest source of personal creativity. Their power in the world is dampened by the bitterness they communicate nonverbally to everyone they meet. A "peace at any price" attitude disguises how badly such women really feel. The natural tenderness and creative intelligence of their caring hearts are numbed by the build-up of pain and confusion.

Cycle of Failure

When we become bitter, we have difficulty living not just with our mates but more importantly with ourselves. A cycle of self-doubt can keep us so worn down that the dream of being equally respected and living a harmonious existence seems meant for someone else, not us. Although divorce has become easier to obtain with less shame attached, the legal system now views the earning power of a woman as nearly equal to that of a man, with potentially devastating consequences. After a divorce, the woman will still carry the emotional responsibility of the children even if the children live in two households. She will frequently assume greater financial responsibility as well, living solely to provide her children with all that she feels they deserve in life. Furthermore, she may be caught in the same psychological struggle with her ex-mate as she was when they were married, the only major difference being her separate household.

While living alone can bring welcome and needed changes, the difficulties a woman experiences with the men in her life will probably continue. Freedom from an insensitive man usually liberates a woman's spirit, but she still needs to unlock the beast to know fully who she is, and to enable healthier choices in future situations and with future mates.

Awakening the Beast Within

The beast in you has many possible faces: bitterness, righteousness, blaming, denying, fearfulness, frustration, envy, and even gushing sweetness. The beast only becomes a useful and constructive part of your personality when you face her most destructive qualities.

If you have been afraid of your beast and covered her up with private feelings of hurt, anger and despair, then now is the time to discover her usefulness in your life. Imagine that your beast has taken back the controls. She is unlimited in power and can do absolutely anything she sets her mind to. She will be watchful of you, ensuring that you don't sink back into a constricted existence. Your beast will lead you through all of your hidden fears to a new, liberated place. She is your very best friend and will nibble away at your consciousness until you awaken to the truth.

Jane

Jane stood in the corner of the bathroom shivering, a towel wrapped around her damp body. A torrent of confused emotions washed over her as Hank, standing against the opposite wall, launched his verbal attack. "Here we go again," she thought, "He's cornered me. I'm vulnerable, naked, and I can't respond."

Jane was afraid of her husband. Once in the past he had lost control, and that memory had become a powerful leash on her anger. She was furious to think that he had this much control over her willingness to express herself in a heated moment.

What started out as a discussion over which account they would use to cover their remodeling project ended up as a heated debate. He wanted to use money that he'd earned before they married. She felt threatened by this because, in her mind, it would make the house more his than hers, and she wanted to feel secure in her own home. There were many other ways to finance the remodeling. The real reason Hank set things up this way was so that he would have control and, ultimately, should they end up divorcing, more rights to the house than she.

"If we get a divorce, this is my house, not yours. You were poor when I met you and you'll be poor when you leave." His vicious comment was a stab right through her heart. Years of care and commitment to their ten-year-old son, and financial contributions rendered through hard work and determination, added up to nothing in his eyes. Once again he had undermined her safety and trust. How could he expect her to agree to sign a financial document when she had very little security emotionally? All she could think about was what a hypocrite he was, paying lip service to his pride in her (always to other people) and using such cruel and immature tactics to get his way behind the scenes. The irony was that he did not know how much damage he was doing in this moment and he was completely out of touch with his need to control her and keep her in a submissive place.

Jane turned to the mirror, her husband's voice fading as she focused on her naked self. Then, as she appraised her image with unprecedented honesty, something magical happened: In the mirror, she saw strength and courage. Jane realized there was nothing to fix — but there was something to do. "You don't deserve to be treated this way, Jane. Stop waiting for him to change. Change yourself — risk something!"

When she stopped herself from slipping into a reactive state, Jane's fierceness came forward like a beast at her behest.

Turning calmly to look at Hank, she said, "You are undermining my trust in you and the consequences are great should this pattern continue." As she walked past him, Hank's mouth dropped open in shock. She had not been reactive at all. Instead a laser beam had radiated from her feet to the top of her head, empowering her with strength and true integrity. This was how she really felt and it was far more effective than fear. Something in Jane had awakened.

Gina

It was easy for Gina to turn into a crazed woman when her husband Kevin used his passive tactics on her. He was always undermining her authority with the children in deceptive, seemingly innocent ways. Here she was again, stuck in the middle of a dead-end situation. He just refused to be cooperative with her on the most important issues where their kids were concerned. She always ended up looking bad while he came out smelling like a rose. What really was going on, Gina surmised, was that Kevin was angry with her and unable to communicate his feelings directly. Instead he tried to reach her in passive ways such as crippling her effectiveness with the children. He knew exactly the things that upset her and did them anyway. Every time, it seemed, she bit the bait and reacted in outrage.

How Gina longed for Kevin to tell her about his feelings when something upset him. She thought of all the times she'd foolishly let him trap her in this way and how every time her trust and openness towards him had diminished. "What a stupid game to be playing, yet I continue to participate. He gets to me every time!"

Gina found herself slipping into a dreamy state. She saw herself in a distant place — in an atmosphere of calm where she could view herself and her reactions differently. Gina decided to do something very unusual for her — relinquish all control to Kevin. She would go away for the weekend by herself and let him do everything his way. For a weekend, she would not remind, organize, pay attention to, cuddle, nurture, or parent anyone. "Let's see where things are on Monday afternoon when I come back," Gina thought.

Kevin was outraged at her leaving, but Gina had to go — something had to change. While away, Gina allowed her beast to emerge and realized the depths of her rage. She pulled a pillow off the hotel-room sofa, imagined that it was Kevin and yelled, screamed and raged about the negative traits that caused her so much anger. Then, she wrote down all of her feelings and took stock of her past, reviewing memories of how her parents had treated her and of things that made her angry in childhood, adolescence and her early twenties. It became apparent to Gina that feeling out-of-control had a haunting familiarity. Growing up at home she had experienced this same emotional state on a regular basis. Her father had demonstrated a passive, controlling personality much like Kevin's — always undermining her mother's authority. On some level, Gina felt undeserving and she had to face those feelings in order to confront her beast. Gina knew that it was up to her to change her relationship with Kevin, and this was the first step. She awakened.

Marta

Marta had been denied the opportunity to say how she really felt throughout thirty-seven years of marriage to Jorge. Every time she opened up and did her best to communicate from a non-defensive position about her feelings, Jorge managed to control the entire situation. When it came to having her feelings heard and understood, their exchanges were never complete. There was no room to share deep, intimate feelings because Jorge always had to be "right." His rage and competitive nature made it impossible for Marta to open up.

During arguments, Jorge always managed to turn things around by using his most aggressive tactics to get her to accept his terms. "Look what I've done for you" was his favorite line. His selfishness and manipulations were constant. When Jorge was growing up, he was everyone's object of adoration. Unfortunately, he learned very early that through emotional manipulation he could almost always get his way. He did not like boundaries at all. In fact, he celebrated the fact that he had led a wild life prior to his marriage, often saying to Marta, "I was happy before I met you, and I'll be happy without you."

Marta was deeply saddened by the realization that Jorge had existed without her for many years, even though they lived in the same household. The door to her heart had shut a long time ago. But still a feeling of love for him confused her and kept her in the relationship.

Marta's children were grown and she found her job increasingly unsatisfying, so she decided to challenge herself. Her survival was not at stake anymore — she could make it on her own, even if she changed jobs. She felt a longing to wake up to parts of herself that she had lost, and the only way for her to do that was to gain more understanding of herself — to face her beast, take chances she had put off for years and risk knowing who she really was by doing the things she dreamed of.

When Marta buried her mother, who had led a similar life, the event catapulted Marta to a new level of self-examination. She wrote a vision statement outlining how she wanted the rest of her life to look. She felt a flood of relief just imagining the changes she would make. For the next two years, Marta would concentrate on developing a relationship with herself, something she had never before done. The most important first step was to dive into the well of feelings she had been storing deep inside. Marta was afraid, but I reassured her: Her beast would help. She closed her eyes and imagined herself twice her size, aggressive and vocal, a powerful beast fiercely communicating her likes and dislikes and stating her intentions. Then, when she opened her eyes, she wrote down all of the ways she planned to change: She would gain skill in communicating with her partner, learn to express how she wanted to be perceived and treated, and she would really believe that she deserved a new level of respect and intimacy. These were big steps for Marta.

Drawing Out Your Beast

The way to draw out your beast is to know that she is a powerful force in your life. Whatever your beast feels, wherever she hurts or is shut-down, serves as a point of reference as you start to create change. In this regard, it is necessary as a beginning step to identify all of the places where the beast lives, what she looks like, what kind of expression she has — especially when challenged — and why she feels the way she does. The more you can identify with the beast in you, the more you'll be able to use her healing power to change your life. The beast must be recognized.

As long as your beast goes unacknowledged, you will experience an extreme absence of power. Your hurt could be just below the surface sucking power. It could be masking anger. Your hurt could build and build to the point where, unknowingly, you operate out of fear. Many women find themselves reacting this way and don't know why. The ultimate loss of power is to fear that you'll be rejected. The irony is, you are *continually* being rejected. *You* are rejecting parts of the beast that you need to understand and heal. In response, your partner rejects those parts of you that are powerful and beautiful. When you draw out and heal those parts, your partner will see and respond to you differently.

The following exercise will help you begin a relationship with the beast in you. If it feels silly or awkward, don't worry. Many women feel this way. It is hard for some of us to identify with a part of ourselves that feels almost masculine. Repeat the exercise on a regular basis. Every time you feel stuck or confused about a situation involving your mate, the beast will help you to become aware of your feelings.

The heart prayer serves as a completion. Following the exercise, after you've emptied out the negative energy, use the heart prayer to fill the emptiness with love.

✣✦ Exercise: ✦✣
Who Is Your Beast?

Using the opposite hand from the one with which you usually write, describe what your beast looks like. Using this hand will help free you from your analytical side and challenge you to open a different door. As you write, move your judgmental urges out of the way — send them to the back of your mind and allow your thoughts to flow freely.

Answer the following questions:
- What does the beast look like when she is hurt or angry, sad or rejected, confused or lonely?
- Where does the beast live? Describe the emotional environment in as much detail as you can.
- What incidents that occur daily with your love partner bring out the beast?

List the ways that your beast has given away her power, and to whom she has given it. Ideas from the past, from your relationships with other men or your father may emerge. You may see a common thread. Write about specific incidents in as much detail as possible.

To find out what is draining your power, complete these sentences:
Every time I...   the beast...
In the past, when I have tried to be powerful and allow my strength to come forward, the beast in me...
The beast in me feels powerless when...
When my love partner...

The spell can only be broken if you welcome the beast like a guest into your heart space and allow her to sit there, looking out into the world with eyes of her own. The next time your partner angers, criticizes, irritates, or confuses you and you are aware of this dark energy inside, draw out the beast. Let the beast expose your hidden conflicts and the hurt that lies beneath your actions. You have probably been ignoring some fierce emotions sitting at the base of your being that only the beast knows and understands.

♥ **Heart Prayer:** *I am able to retrieve my lost power by embracing fully all that I am. When I remove the limits on my ideas about myself, the growth I experience transforms my life. Everything I need to know is within the darkness and the light.*

Another way to embrace your beast is to observe the beast in your partner. It may be difficult to understand how his beast could have anything to do with yours, but try it out and see where it takes you. Give yourself permission to experiment with new ideas. Remember, the more you take full responsibility for your dark force, the more healing potential you have.

The next exercise will take you deeper into your beast. If answers are not immediate, that's okay — come back to the exercise at another time.

✺ *Exercise:* ✺
Becoming the Beast

Write your answers to these questions in as much detail as possible:
- What about your wounded man troubles you most? What do you strongly dislike? Make a complete list. Try not to judge your responses. Star the items that affect you most negatively — the qualities, behaviors, or habits that you really detest.
- What have you tried not to be or become?
- What compulsions, addictions, or distressing thoughts exist in your secret life?

(continued)

- In order to survive and be secure, what have you decided you must do or be?
- When do you experience exaggerated emotions with your mate? What things that he says or does bother you most?
- What have you shoved down deep inside that you now recognize is a legitimate part of you?
- What lies behind your vengeful feelings and your desire to hold onto past resentments?
- What might be underneath your anger, criticisms, fears, insecurities, arrogance and hurts?

♥ **Heart Prayer:** *Beside and inside my beast is my power and wisdom. I have the courage to feel and own the part of me that I have denied for so long. In this way I truly love myself, and can more fully love my partner.*

Something comes back to you when you are ready to look deeply into what and who you are. The beast has lived in you for a long time, collecting all the garbage along the way. You and your beast are allies. Your beast always tells the truth about your life. You may not like it, but the part of your beast that frightens you most also represents the area with the highest readiness for growth.

By owning what you fear, you harness its intensity.

Owning what you fear means telling yourself how rotten you could be if you let those qualities out.

In the imperfections of your partner, you find your own imperfections and a pathway to perfection.

You have the power to cross over to a new place. You cannot overpower and control your beast, you must befriend her, as you must be willing to befriend your partner's beast. You must acknowledge your beast as part of you. Making peace with her will take you over the bridge into a new existence.

Your beast will be transformed into raw energy — powerful and beautiful — and will lead you to extraordinary experiences. She will never go away. When you decide to face your beast, you — and the man in your life — will change.

Your worth is hidden in the beast. When you find it, your partner will find it!

Healing Your Beast

The partner you have attracted into your life can take you into the far reaches of your unconscious so that you may truly know who you are. Somewhere in you is a desire to understand. Underneath your judgment, criticism and pain is a deep longing for this truth. It is to this part of you that I speak now: When you live in pain your spirit dies. The beast dominates and controls your life — you do not. The following are some important steps to help you make peace:

- Talk with the beast within you. Ask what you need from her to make peace. Listen with your heart, not your mind. Don't try to analyze what you hear or interpret the meaning right away. Let it sit in your subconscious and do its own work.
- Put on the mask of the beast's suffering. Allow the ugliness to come through. Be willing to identify your private envies and jealousies. They will lead you to the rage that the beast in you feels.
- Feel the beast, experience her, be willing to go right into her suffering. Go all the way inside her raw energy where there are no words, only feelings. If you can, allow yourself to be consumed by this energy — get all resistance out of the way.

While every part of you may be resisting this idea, it is important to acknowledge that your beast has been with you for a very long time. Open your whole being to the parts of yourself that you have denied, discounted, defended, refused, neglected and rejected.

In my case, I had to courageously own and talk to the part of me that wanted sexual freedom. I had to feel the raw, lustful energies within that were capable of luring a man to me and using him for my own satisfaction, nothing more. I put on the mask and allowed my selfish beast to come through. I saw the moment in my past when I adopted this negative trait from my father and took it deep inside me.

When you make peace with your beast — the one inside of you — your creative life will ripen fully. You will begin to feel the value of your mature, true self. In time you will learn to trust all that you are. More importantly, infinite spaces within your consciousness will open up. In this light, a new path will appear. A vision of possibilities will present itself to you and automatically you will reorganize your life, seeing potential everywhere.

3
How Boundaries Heal

There are two ways of meeting difficulties. You alter the difficulties or you alter yourself to meet them.
—Phyllis Bottome

Women are compelled almost biologically to view the world in terms of relationships. We instinctively reach out to one another. In contrast, the men in our lives are compelled to view their world in terms of tasks, power and achievement. They are defensive and aggressive. Well-armored and defended men strike one another emotionally without a second thought.

To love a difficult man while protecting your own continuing growth as a woman, it is essential to develop boundary-setting skills. Only through such skills can you shield your virgin heart from the insensitive emotional brutality of a wounded male. This chapter teaches skills that can turn a difficult man's criticism, thoughtless comments, and immature behavior into harmless acts. Your difficult man's emotional outbursts become windows through which you see into his wounded core, rather than spears that penetrate your caring heart.

One of the most daunting requirements a woman faces is setting boundaries with her difficult man. At every seminar I present, this issue is the burning one. For me, the most difficult are the little boundaries, such as saying no when every part of me is afraid of what he will do when I don't succumb to his wishes. Because I grew up in a home where my father's actions were never outwardly questioned, the intensity involved in challenging my partner is overwhelming to me at times. I have to let the past die, and wake up to the power I have in the present.

In her book, *Possessing the Secret of Joy*, Alice Walker affirms that resistance is the secret of joy for women who have been oppressed. Without fear holding me back, or definitions and perceptions blocking my road, a clarity of thought and action drives me to places I never dreamed possible. Small steps become giant leaps.

Setting boundaries involves more than saying no. We often take on our mate's woundedness. We don't realize how much of his pain and suffering we accept as ours. An open, sensitive woman can become depressed by immersing herself, through empathy, in her mate's emotional ordeals. If he is pained by something in his life, she often can't help feeling what he is feeling. What he is going through has absolutely nothing to do with her, but she may describe herself as "slipping" into despair and feeling "out of control" when mired in her mate's pain. He doesn't have to utter a word. A woman can become so attuned to her mate's emotional pain that she feels it flowing from his core. Her loving heart sees into him, and recognizes his anguish. She loses her boundaries.

Consider the extreme empathic response of a lovely down-to-earth woman named Inga. While on her way to the airport with her new boyfriend of six months, Inga suddenly became aware of a desperate sinking feeling as he related to her incidents involving his children from a previous marriage. She tuned into the deep pain he felt about losing them and, by the end of the ride, was a basket case. On her way home in the car, alone, Inga tried to figure out why she felt such despair, and suddenly remembered a dream she had had the week before. In vivid color, she had dreamt her ex-husband was in her home, occupying a room that she loved. He was motioning for her to come and join him in that room. In the dream, she felt depressed and lost. She looked closely at the inside of his left arm, and saw bright yellow push pins stuck in gaping wounds that extended from his wrist to his shoulder and around into his heart. Then he started chasing her, and attempted to put a yellow push pin into her arm. Inga screamed for her daughter. The scream was real, and she awoke.

Inga recalled that her ex-husband had never shared any feelings with her and was completely out of touch with his own anger and despair. Her marriage had been unfulfilling and "empty," in her words. Her new love, by contrast, shared everything and was quite aware of himself. Inga awoke again, this time to a profound insight: She needed to set emotional boundaries for herself. Being empathic did not mean taking her lover's wounds as her own. Later, in talking with me, Inga redefined love as emotional goodness flowing from her heart to the one she loved, with boundaries in place to maintain her own integrity.

You cannot control your mate; he will do whatever he does. But you do have the power to regain control of yourself. When you pay more attention to past experiences than you do to your power to effect change in the future, you guarantee failure.

Your energy can be entirely blocked by memories of past hurt and fear of future consequences.

You must come to the edge of your feelings, and stand firm in your limits.

Decide what you want and need, and be willing to back yourself up. You may feel uneasy, even terrified, with what you must say or do to make your life more comfortable, but if intuition is calling you to do it, don't ignore those feelings. You have an individual right and responsibility to respond to your deepest voice. When you do express your needs and are on the edge of a new experience, don't be disappointed when your partner comes back at you with resistance. Remember to bring the solid aspects of your personality to bear in these moments and you will prevail, even if you are afraid.

One woman described feeling helpless when her husband verbally attacked her son by a previous marriage, belittling him in front of their other children. While the husband deserved to be cut some slack in his role as a step-parent, he had no right to subject this boy to regular and overt hostility while doting on his other children. My client finally told her husband that if he engaged in any more verbal assaults on her son, she would report him to the child protective services agency. He was horrified, and she felt much stronger for taking a stand.

Make the statement, "I am going to..." instead of asking for permission. Decide on your worth in the relationship, and your mate will reflect that back to you eventually. He may act confused. He may go kicking and screaming into every change, but you have a right to trust your instincts and wishes.

Embrace the fact that negative consequences often precede positive outcomes. Expect these consequences and, when they happen, you'll be prepared.

You may be judging yourself unconsciously prior to every move. Without your realizing it, many of your decisions, or lack thereof, may be fear-based. When you decide to set a limit, you may be logically calculating the reaction before taking action, which only serves to keep you out of touch with what you need and want.

If You Are at the End of Your Rope, Get an Emotional Divorce

In my countless conversations with women who have lived through years of frustration with a partner unwilling to make changes, I have seen "emotional divorces" work miracles. These women haven't quite reached the point of wanting to leave altogether, but they have realized the need for dramatic change.

By unplugging yourself from the continuous current of unhealthy emotional wiring between you and your mate, you create a vacuum, a void that can be filled with new behaviors.

Mary Ellen's story demonstrates the power of the emotional divorce. A 33-year-old high-school teacher, hard working and committed to her job, Mary Ellen gave a great deal of loving energy and guidance to her kids at school. She complained that her partner, Jed, intimidated her continuously. She described this scene: "I was on the telephone, doing business, and he interrupted me with a question he considered important. As it turned out, the urgent thing he needed to ask me had nothing to do with the present moment and could easily have waited until I was off the phone. His interruption was rude and unreasonable."

Jed's narcissism and self-centered behavior created real problems in their marriage. His attitude was, "There is nothing in the world more important than what I do because, financially, I contribute more than you do to the marriage." He had all kinds of justifications for his behavior.

For years Mary Ellen allowed this unbalanced dynamic to continue. As she began to earn more money and receive more recognition in the world, she gained greater self-worth. Nevertheless, the situation became more and more intolerable. Finally she said to me, "I still love my husband very much, but he is not growing in this area. I have tried to demand more respect, but his negative self-centered behavior is overwhelming me." I asked Mary Ellen to speculate as to where her husband might have learned this behavior. She revealed that he was an only child who thought the world revolved around him, and acknowledged that for years she had reinforced this belief by causing her world to revolve around him — a stance that no longer served her.

Mary Ellen felt that the only way she could stay in the relationship was by doing something dramatically different. That's when I introduced the concept of getting an emotional divorce. These were the guidelines:

1. In your heart, remain open and loving toward him as a person.
2. Recognize all of the qualities that you like and that drew you to him in the first place.
3. When your partner behaves in a hurtful or disrespectful way, pull back. Refuse to react or let what is happening affect you.
4. Review the experience in private and validate your response. If you need to, write down the details of the incident.
5. As time passes, you will notice a shift in his response. Because you are not reacting to him as you did in the past, he will start to view you differently.
6. Don't expect a quick resolution. The dynamic between the two of you took years to form and will require time to unravel.

In Mary Ellen's case, when her husband behaved in self-centered ways, she simply gave him a blank stare. She noticed that she gradually became calmer in these moments, which bolstered her ability to respond to him assertively. When on the phone, she would pause and say, "I realize you have something to tell me, and I'll be with you in just a moment." The first few times she did this, he yelled at her or walked off angrily. She reported that she didn't care. Changes were occurring that gave her strength in the face of behavior that had long been troublesome. Getting emotionally divorced from the painful and difficult issues allowed the good to grow and the bad to be buried.

This formula may not work for everyone, but in many cases it creates more room for change.

We are complex creatures, and when faced with new information, we learn. Remember that your problems, whatever they are, presented themselves so that you can grow in love, beginning with yourself. You have the capacity to overcome your own feelings of inadequacy and teach those around you to honor and respect you. It is no small task, but it can be done. Your mate mirrors to you what you must learn. You attracted these problems in order to master new lessons. Take advantage of the opportunity. In the right moment, sit down with your partner and tell him how you feel about what is happening between the two of you. Tell him specifically how you want to be treated and, without making him the bad guy, enroll him in change.

✄ *Exercise:* ✄
Setting a Boundary

Complete the following sentences:
- A boundary I have been wanting to set is...
- The reason I haven't is...
- My motivation for setting this boundary is...

(continued)

- I am afraid that if I set this boundary, he will...
- If I set this boundary, I'm afraid I will lose...
- A place I have set boundaries successfully in the past is...
- That success makes me feel...

Invite into your heart the image of your goal and ask that higher guidance prepare you to manifest this goal.

♥ **Heart Prayer:** A gentle presence leads me through my fear.

Don't Turn on Yourself

A common reaction women have to their pain is to turn the negativity inward. Often, when the relationship struggle is worsening, and there are no obvious signs of improvement, women redirect their hurtful and angry feelings toward their own center. When they are not getting anywhere, they take their frustration out on themselves through self-negation, "if-only's," and feelings of failure. If this is something you tend to do, retrain yourself. Learn to be gentle with yourself regarding unresolved issues. Take a more confident stand. Trust that the situation will eventually be worked out.

Another way that you may react to the unresolved conflicts in your relationship is to slip into comfortable but self-destructive behavior patterns. Overeating, overworking, excessive drinking, engaging in casual sexual encounters, or becoming over-controlling are typical of the ways in which we cross our own boundaries. Perhaps you have a compulsion or two in your secret life. When you engage in this compulsive behavior, you are turning against yourself. It is far more effective to keep the focus on the truth of your pain, anger and confusion. This allows you to have a beginning, middle and end to the conflicts within you and then get back to taking a stand with your partner. If you were out in the street without an umbrella and it began to rain heavily, you would seek shelter or cover your head with a newspaper or plastic bag. You wouldn't stand in the rain getting soaked and wail, "I'm such a jerk for not remembering my umbrella."

The Ultimate Boundary

Leaving is the ultimate boundary. It is also the hardest decision that a woman can make. When you contemplate the shattered dream and the complexities of your life, leaving a relationship portends tremendous consequences. No one knows more than you what a heart-wrenching decision this is. Sometimes the pain and lack of fulfillment are so great, however, that the decision to leave is the right one. If, in your heart, you know that you will be hurt more by staying in the marriage, then you must place the biggest boundary of all between you and your partner — you must leave.

When a woman in counseling agonizes over the decision to leave her mate, I usually ask her to look at the price she is paying by staying in a situation that hurts her heart, her self-esteem, her growth and her happiness. Many women make the choice to leave their relationships because they feel stuck and can't seem to move in any direction but out.

Setting this ultimate boundary can create real problems though, especially if your partner has never honored boundaries while you've been together. The same dynamic may continue when you are separated, as in the following example.

Liddy had a three-year-old son. Her wealthy husband, Bret, traveled frequently and had various business projects around town that kept him thoroughly occupied, so Liddy was the primary caregiver in the relationship. Somewhat against her will, Liddy had signed a prenuptial agreement with Bret. He had thrown down the papers the day before their wedding and said, "Here, just sign these. My family won't be comfortable unless we get this out of the way before we tie the knot." Four months pregnant and eager to have their baby, Liddy signed the document. She had a horrible feeling in her gut, but she didn't listen to herself.

Bret felt perfectly justified in setting his boundary with Liddy before they married. Liddy was saddened and angry at the way it was handled. That pattern continued throughout the marriage. Where boundaries were concerned, Bret had no trouble communicating his needs to Liddy, but Liddy remained mute about her needs.

After the first couple of years, Bret started to become more withholding and distant from Liddy. She could sense a big change in him and suspected that he was sleeping around. Then Liddy caught Bret in a situation that had all the earmarks of reckless infidelity. Arriving home early from a class, Liddy found her husband in bed naked. Two glasses of wine were sitting on the twin night stands. She heard shuffling and the sound of a door closing down the hallway. Suddenly it hit her — the person scurrying down the hallway was their nanny. Liddy was crazed with anger. She was never able to prove that anything happened — both parties denied it — but the marriage was finished. After repeated efforts to get Bret involved in counseling, all rebuffed, Liddy demanded a divorce.

When Liddy moved into her new home, she decided that setting boundaries was extremely important, especially since she had never set them during her marriage. The need for boundaries became starkly apparent the first time Bret arrived to pick up their little boy. Liddy opened the door and Bret walked right in, used the bathroom, looked around the house, peered into the refrigerator and basically acted as if he owned the place. Liddy was so accustomed to this kind of behavior that she saw nothing wrong with it at first. Later, she realized that it was intolerable.

In counseling, Liddy decided on a boundary-setting strategy and we talked through all the different possible scenarios. She felt relieved to be able to draw a healthy line between herself and Bret. Liddy asked Bret to respect her privacy and her space. She knew that he would still try to break the rules, so she met him at the door on visitation days and refused to let him enter the house. Bret was enraged over this treatment, and Liddy found it very hard to persist. But she did, and with repeated assertive acts, began to feel more powerful. For Liddy, knowing she had her life back was the key.

Negative Control

Negative control is what we assert when we play a particular role to ensure that things stay the way we wish them — familiar, easy, unchallenged, but always restricted to what is familiar to us. Our motivation is not to be liberated, but to remain in ignorance, bondage and pain.

The use of negative control can result in crippling effects. Define your motives carefully when you are setting a boundary with your mate. Be sure that you are not acting from a survival mode. If you recognize fear and insecurity as your motives for controlling him, then plunge into those fears. In your imagination, go through the worst-case scenario. Live it — actually see it happening in your mind's eye. When you are finished, let it die. For example, if you are afraid he will leave you, then imagine his leaving and see it all the way through. This fear could be motivating your behavior. Subtle things you say or do could be representations of the fear. Trust that you'll live through it, because you will. Harness your spiritual strength to support you in giving up what no longer serves you.

The Healing Boundary

Your life is nourished by the continual healing you experience. This is the most important food for your soul. A healing boundary is one that demonstrates how loving you are to yourself; it is where you truly gauge your growth. For example, consider the boundary you place on yourself when you wish to accomplish something. Perhaps you wish to get work done at home, so you don't answer phone calls. Maybe you tell those who interrupt you at work to schedule a time to talk with you instead of barging in expecting you to respond. These are obvious situations that you face in your daily life.

You must also create some not-so-obvious boundaries deep within yourself. These boundaries begin when you make a decision and remember what you know to be right for you. Perhaps the boundary is emotional in nature — something that will force you to move in the right direction. For example, you might decide to stop yourself when you become aware that you are using tactics to avoid rather than confront something negative in your life. Boundaries are meant to heal and help you get beyond ineffective behavior. They are meant to break the chains of inertia and help you overcome any repression that is going on inside or outside.

As each day dawns, you must challenge yourself by looking at your last stand and reaching beyond it. Your partner is your reference, always showing what is next, but you are the active participant who needs to take the actual step. Every time you stand by your own convictions, you heal a part of your past. You reclaim something that was lost and inject power into the line that you drew. This becomes your support as you prepare to take the next stand, ever strengthening and increasing your ability to be effective in the world and especially with your love partner.

Put a Boundary Around Your Heart

Imagine your emotional heart. See it functioning beautifully. You've heard the expression, "My heart is happy." So, visualize a thriving, happy emotional heart inside of you, overflowing with goodness. Your heart deserves protection from the outside world, from all the negative elements with which it comes in contact. Your heart is a power source. Moment to moment, it gives you security and inner peace. Visualize a boundary of light surrounding all this goodness, protecting you from unpleasant and unhealthy behavior in your partner.

A broken heart comes from being violated, hurt, betrayed, let down and disappointed in relationships. While you still have healing to do, your heart deserves to be protected from everyday emotional turmoil. Put a boundary around your heart and protect yourself from further violations.

Exercise: Healing Steps

Imagine that you have complete control of your life. Everything works and feels positive. With a clear mind, envision a great path before you. Beauty surrounds you as you stand before gigantic steps that lead you to a crystal mound. At the top of this mound is a radiant building filled with light. The structure glows with vibrant energy. You long to go there, sensing that it contains infinite love — all you have ever wanted or needed. Look down at the first step and identify exactly what it is. Look honestly at your life. What can you do on this beautiful path that will lead you to more love? The step may be challenging. It may seem difficult to take, but you can do it if you let yourself. Care enough, have enough faith to take this healing step. When you do, you will find the energy and spiritual esteem to take the next step, and the next. Take back the power you

(continued)

have lost in your life. Claim your lost property. Only you can know what it is. This is the edge you want. This is where your passion and fire exist. If you are afraid, embrace your fear and move onto the step. Declare yourself, stand up for your ideal and trust the future to supply you with what you want and need in your life. Say to yourself, "I have no limitations. I can't be tied down by myself or anyone else. I unbind my hands and heart and set myself completely free to take action."

♥ **Heart Prayer:** My responsibility is to identify my next healing step. I wait in anticipation to know.

✎ Exercise: ✎
Leave It in a Basket

This exercise will help you to take the next step, which is to set a boundary for yourself.

In writing, describe an argument that you and your partner have been having for a long time. Put down all of your feelings from beginning to end, with as much detail as possible. The exercise of writing is very important as a way of validating all of your emotions, so be sure to take time to do this part. Put this document in an envelope and mark the date on the outside. If you have used a word processing program, create a computer file using the date. Place the envelope in a basket in your cupboard or desk or inside a computer directory labeled, "Unfinished Business."

You are not denying yourself by filing your thoughts away. You are simply leaving the issue for a time, knowing that you will come back to it in the near future when your heart has had a chance to rest. You are preserving good energy and refusing to indulge in wasted discussion.

♥ **Heart Prayer:** May a divine perception intervene and guide me to a higher resolution.

Imagine the Ideal to Create Something Real

Many of us are out of touch with the range of possibilities available in our lives. We need to learn to draw from our rich imagination to bring forth the things we want.

Take the limits off your thinking. By imagining something ideal, you will have a goal, a target. For example, make a list of ideal qualities that you would like your mate to share with you in intimacy. If you never expect it, you'll certainly never get it. The key is to imagine what you want and then expect it with a feeling of deservedness rather than control. For example, you might write, "I am worthy of having a man who wants to know what I feel about things, who is passionately interested in my point of view. My ideal lover demonstrates excitement and a sense of intrigue when I have something deep and intimate to share."

Open your heart to a new and beautiful relationship. Then leave this image tucked in the back of your mind as an ideal and say "yes" to it once in a while.

Visualize in your mind's eye an ideal way of being. Write down your thoughts. For example, here is my visualization of the ideal relationship:

With an open heart, I feel divine forces at work all of the time. My relationship is not something I need, but something that leads me to my highest state of being. Each time I am challenged, I acknowledge the challenge as a lesson necessary for growth. I am overjoyed to learn the lesson because it will allow me to be all that I can be.

I feel safe deep inside. The safety comes from the light that burns brightly at my core. When I look at the light, I know who I am, separate from my partner. The light gives me strength to face the truth of my life and respond according to the highest good for all concerned.

The passion that moves through me is like an invisible flow of energy ignited by divine forces. It is spiritual energy that remains constant, keeping me integrated and whole. I am boundless in my potential to love and be loved, to grow individually and with my lover.

I have discovered a new reality far beyond that which words can express. This new reality is hidden behind the force of my life. I look for clues to bring it into the open, and heal what must be healed. When I come upon a wall that threatens to interrupt the flow of love between me and my partner, I look deeply into the truth at the center of my being and find a way to bring the wall all the way down. I am liberating myself from all that I fear, giving myself permission to reach into my brilliant and talented self.

Every day I discover more of me. I acknowledge my relationship as a testing ground that allows me to go further out into the world to discover and create magic. I am present and invoking love and light always. A blazing energy flows through me, showing me how to love every second of my life.

4

The Power of a Tender, Caring Heart

You have to have great heart to see with this kind of vision. How do you get such a heart? You recognize your worth, you know what you really are, you know what you contain within yourself.
—Swami Chidvilasananda
Everything Happens for the Best: A Book of Contemplations

When you have claimed your beast and declared it an important part of you, the vital energy of your caring heart will emerge. You must know the power of your caring heart in order to use that power to heal your relationship. The caring heart is a feminine force. It feels much — at times flooded with tears and anguish, holding the sorrow of the world and simultaneously experiencing longings and desires born of life's every breath. It is from the core of the caring heart that new life emerges, like a birth, as love permeates sorrow and the purest ideas come forth.

For those of us who have grown up believing that we have a duty to ourselves, our daughters, our sisters, and our mothers, the most acute need is that we declare our spiritual independence. That is the one thing over which we always have control. Spiritual esteem comes from learning to depend on a deeper truth. When we have spiritual esteem, we rely less on short-term thinking and hold out for the big "aha's" that eventually present themselves. If we can learn to stand apart and detach ourselves from the overwhelming emotional needs of our partners, we can love them not only when they are being open and receiving our love but when they are stuck in despair, confusion, and anger. They have a right to work out their issues as much as we have a right to work out ours. We will always outdistance them in our desire for growth, because our genetic makeup causes us to long for emotional connectedness. While men also seek intimacy, they must learn to overcome social conditioning that teaches them to compete, to fight for what they want, to win. In love, there are no winners, only differences to embrace and enjoy. Neither are there mistakes. Every single incident is a point of reference on the map that guides us to our love potential.

You will fully realize the power of your caring heart as you embrace the multidimensional aspects of a deeper love for yourself. This is the source from which your power emanates. This is where you find all your needs and wants and are able to express and actualize them.

Your Loving Intention

Intention is where it all begins. Intention is stronger than will because it can be set into action instantly. Even if your will was crushed at an early age, your intention will give you strength. It is through loving intention that loving choices are made and devotion expressed. Without loving intention, change does not occur. First and foremost, you must know that you have the power of love in your heart. When you do, intention will provide the follow-through. The benefits that will accrue to your relationships are extraordinary. Intention is what ends disputes and breaks down the walls of fear, mistrust and misunderstanding that separate individuals, groups, and nations. Intention is the tool with which our hearts dig down to places where the walls are thick with confusion and pain. Intention is as basic to lasting relationships as the earth is to the tree that grows from it.

Heaven within is dependent on the food of your intention, which is driven by your power. Always use power for your own growth. Others will feel its ripple and grow with you. Use intention to direct your power and allow it to lead you to the next chapter of life.

Loving intention — the active, positive use of your heart's energy — always leads to resolution.

The good upon which you place your attention grows stronger and leads to resolution. You speed up your spiritual growth when you put loving intention before all other concerns. When you focus here you find purpose.

Often, the emptiness that we feel inside is directly related to lack of direction and purpose in our lives. If we supply the intention to love, suddenly our purpose becomes clear. We have a place to go!

All of the great spiritual teachers show us that loving intention is the key to unlocking and using the full powers of the heart. It never fails to open a door. You will be loved back when loving intention guides your actions. You multiply the gifts of the heart by one-hundred every time you operate from this potent position. Instead of a loss of physical energy, which is what many women feel when they are put down, dumped on, or attacked in some way, you experience an increase in both emotional and physical energy when you direct the negative force away from you and focus your intention to love and heal on the source of negativity. While it may feel like a leap in the dark, what have you got to lose but a moment in the unknown?

Don't try to meddle in your mate's psyche. If you try to manipulate him through less than direct loving, he will become defensive and distant and attack you at every turn.

☙ *Exercise:* ❧
The Power of Caring

The caring heart is more powerful than any physical force on earth. Scientific studies have proven that open, loving behaviors not only reduce stress in the individual who does the loving, but in those who receive the love. Your love has bioenergetic energy. It projects a magnetic charge, creating a positive field around the person to whom you direct it.

The following two-step technique reveals the power in the caring heart. Go through the process once using only your imagination. Then, implement the process when you are in a difficult situation with your partner.

Step 1: Imagine that your partner is angry and acting in a hostile or fearful way. Perhaps he is lashing out at you verbally or sending you raging vibrations through his behavior. The goal is to protect yourself from this aggressive energy, at the same time staying open and loving.

Directly in front of your heart, imagine a flowing river that takes all of the anger away. You must be patient and wait as the rage quiets down and negative emotions are spent. As you wait, remain focused on the river protecting your heart. Don't move up to your mind and try to make sense of what is being thrown your way. The information is coming from his wounded heart and can only hurt your heart if you try to explain it. Rational interpretations won't work, so just remain inside of your own loving heart and allow the negative attacks to flow away from you.

Step 2: When all is calm, imagine that your heart has eyes and can see all the way into the soul that hides beneath his anger. Underneath all of the pain and rage is the tender, caring person you fell in love with. The attack has defused his energy, and you are able to look deeply. An old image of love shared between the two of you may float across your visual screen. Keep your seeing heart focused on his. Send him a psychic message of love that reaches him at his core. *Trust that this is happening and remain focused.* The power you have within your heart is beyond imagination, but imagination is needed to build your belief in that power. When you place your attention on your heart's power, rather than feeling defeated and running away emotionally, your love causes changes and growth to occur in you and in your partner. All that you dream of having comes to you through the power of your caring heart.

Remember, it is very important to imagine this experience from beginning to end before actually trying it. Mental rehearsal will give you the confidence you need when you are challenged to use the process in real life.

This process can have profound effects on you, too, leading to a more efficient use of your power. Dramatic and subtle changes occur with repeated use of this technique on your love partner.

♥ **Heart Prayer:** His pain, anger, and aggression belong to him. My heart's energy is best spent in compassion, which allows me to see beyond his hurt into his soul.

Having the Heart to Win

My own experience of transcendence, along with my work assisting clients to access this extraordinary dimension of their psyches, has profoundly affected the approach I use in counseling. Instead of focusing primarily on ways of empowering women to confront male dominance, I have learned to explore a more subtle dynamic. Instead of motivating women to express the power of their anger, I assist women to mobilize the power of transcendent love. This is not to discredit anger as a necessary and important first step; however, unless anger is directed in ways that produce real change, it is often more damaging than it is helpful because the foundation for change is not in place. The beast has anger that must be felt, heard and understood, but it is separate and must be kept apart from the work of the caring heart.

At first I was filled with ambivalence — even subtle dread — as I tested my new approach to relationship counseling. Was I capitulating to male dominance? Formerly, my comfort with my own anger had allowed me to feel justified in motivating women to access their rage. Men who were demeaning, thoughtless, overbearing, and cruel deserved to be on the receiving end of a woman's wrath. But the consequences of confrontation frequently included destruction of the relationship, rather than healing and growth. As a therapist, my goal was to assist women in pain and to help them achieve greater satisfaction within themselves and their relationships. Divorce frequently seemed like a victory.

Paradoxically, I grew to appreciate the value of my new approach to women's relationship counseling through the everyday use of a seldom questioned term in that bastion of male dominance — sports, particularly boxing. When a boxer shows extraordinary courage in a long fight, he is said to have heart. In sports, the sacred temple of testosterone, men recognize the existence of a tapline to energy and power. When men speak of an athlete having the heart to win, they are saying that the athlete cares so much about winning that he (or she) taps into a source of extraordinary courage, energy and determination that carries him through the contest.

The term *heart* is used in other contexts as well. We seem to recognize the primordial nature of forces underlying heart when we speak of a horse having the heart to win. The term connotes more than determination; it suggests a certain wisdom or judgment, as when a businessman describes a competitor as having the "heart to succeed." These uses of the term *heart* imply something approaching reverence for a competitor doing battle. Our male dominated culture seems to casually recognize this spiritually empowered dimension of the psyche — the primordial impulse of caring — at least when it is directed toward using the energy of love.

And what is love? M. Scott Peck defines love quite simply and beautifully in his book *The Road Less Traveled*: "I define love as thus: The will to extend one's self for the purpose of nurturing one's own or another's spiritual growth." Love is self, extended or given. As such, love carries with it everything in our experience. It encompasses our entire history, including all the dark and painful memories we have from birth to the present. Love even includes the decisions we make about what love looks like. My decision was, "Women get their hearts broken by men, and men are not trustworthy." That belief system severely limited my capacity to love. Realizing its limitations produced one of my deepest learnings.

Snared by His Shame

Your heart's capacity for caring is far greater than you've ever dreamed. Many men fear love, because deep inside they believe that to love is to demonstrate weakness. Men mask their vulnerability to avoid feelings of shame. Unacknowledged shame can turn to rage, contributing to an unhealthy alliance with you, the love partner.

When you expose your mate's shame, either through your projections or your own vulnerabilities, he is likely to feel very threatened and may lash out at you in anger. He becomes defensive in order to hide his shame. He must not be found out.

This is not to say that you are exempt from shame. You are

not. However, your shame has a very different face, with features that reflect beliefs about your defectiveness. His shame is related to his own issues, his ideals, his performance in the world or his loss of power and control in life. It has nothing to do with you.

The unconscious factor in shame is overwhelming when it shows up as contempt for you. When he turns the table, you end up feeling powerless, guilty, intimidated, and helpless. All the feelings that lie deep in his unconscious mind, masked by his own shame, are somehow projected onto you. If you feel like a victim in your relationship, it is important to look at whether you are carrying his shame (or his shameless behavior). For example, a rapist feels no shame during or after the act. The victim takes on his shame. If the perpetrator allowed himself to experience appropriate feelings, to own his shame, he could not complete the act.

Your mate's unacknowledged shame gives rise to anger, often rage, and can lead to attacks on you. Unconsciously, he needs to redirect his dark feelings and to keep a tight seal on his hurt heart. He may humiliate or verbally attack you, inflict shame on you, make condescending remarks, withdraw emotionally, blame you, or use sarcasm in humorous but threatening ways to avoid dealing with his real feelings.

Therefore, it is imperative that you attempt to understand his shame. You can do this by looking at him with an objective eye. Give yourself permission to be less reactive and more aware.

He may have many layers of shameful feelings of which he is completely unaware. He may have no sense of guilt or remorse about the consequences of his behavior. To be responsible for his shame he would need to come forward willingly and discuss it. When a man is deeply wounded, feelings of regret are hard to contact. He can't own what he's done or is doing to you because ultimately he would have to own what he's doing to himself. To reach this point requires a self-awareness that he may not have achieved. You have no way of knowing what he might feel ashamed of based on experiences in his past. Know that the shame is there and it is his, not yours. He will recognize it when he is ready.

You can repair and heal your relationship if you are willing to do your work and identify *your* shame. In the moment when you are being attacked, accused or blamed, you will be able to look into yourself and decide where the responsibility lies. Shame only teaches us that we must heal negative feelings about ourselves. By seeking to understand his, and finding yours, you will unlock more of your healing energy.

If you cannot contact any shame, never mind. Perhaps it is beyond language. Plant the seed — eventually it will germinate. Shame is like an invisible barrier that encompasses the heart — that is why it is so hard to see.

For example, it took me many years to see that I had shameful feelings about myself. When I came back to my home at sixteen to visit my parents after having my baby, I walked in the door and my father turned his back on me, as if to shame me. He ignored me the whole time I was there, about forty minutes. I was not conscious that I felt ashamed of myself, but in that moment the message was received and I accepted it as mine.

In actuality, it was his own shame he projected. He turned away from me in anger because he was hurt by what happened and felt ashamed of himself for whatever he had done that caused it. He was unable to sort through and understand why something like that happened. In his own quiet and confusion, he did the only thing he could — he pulled away in shame, projecting that shame onto me.

ᴧᴑ *Exercise:* ᴑᴧ
Finding Your Shame

Step One: Your Shame

You cannot influence the release of his shame. You can only accept it, while you learn more about your own shame. Close your eyes. Imagine a safe love around your heart. One by one, pull out the thoughts you have about shame. Identify anything you feel ashamed of. Look at it in your mind's eye. Own it as yours and then allow it to evaporate in air.

Perhaps you feel ashamed of your body, or a particular behavior pattern, or something you consider a personal failing. Specific incidents in earlier years are the architects of your shame.

By doing this exercise, you determine what is yours. The next time he reacts to you in a negative way, you will have more information about yourself and you will understand how that information relates to the situation at hand.

Step Two: His Shame

When you talk to your mate about your shame, you model intimate communication. For example, this is how I communicated to my husband about my shame, tying it into my experience of him:

When I was very young, perhaps ten, I remember looking at the men in my life — my father, grandfather, and brothers — and noticing that they all treated women the same way, with little respect. I must have done something to deserve this and there must have been something wrong with my mother. I felt angry and ashamed. When I became pregnant at age fifteen, my father rejected me, which confirmed that I was terribly flawed. The world was a confusing place then. I lived in a home with a father who had affairs with other women while heaping verbal and sometimes physical abuse on my mother, and I took on a huge load of shame because of what happened to me. I can see now that I've carried this shame for a long time and I recognize how it has affected our relationship. Because of my own feelings of unworthiness, I have never expected you to be loyal. Perhaps I haven't felt deserving. I know now that I deserve loyalty and that I want it. I'm willing to look deep inside at who I really am and to love that part of me. I want you to feel safe enough to show me the parts of yourself that have caused you shame. It feels really good to talk to you this way.

♥ **Heart Prayer:** I release myself from being the object of his shame. His shame belongs to him, not me. I take responsibility for my own shame and apply it to my healing process.

❧ *Exercise:* ❧
Straight From the Heart

If Cupid were to shoot an arrow into your heart and the arrow were to inject some special power, what would you wish it to be?

Many of you have been so bogged down with your confusing and difficult lives that even the idea of using special healing powers on your mate seems ludicrous. Despite this, you can still dare yourself to discover new and different ways to strengthen your relationship.

What you long for is love. What you deserve is a liberated experience of love. You have come a long way, perhaps already surpassing your previous expectations. You are giving love to yourself at the level you are capable of receiving. The more you receive, the more powerful you become as a love conduit, and as a healer.

You will eventually get the powers you wish for. They might not come in the formula you envision, but they will arrive — through nature's design and through your focus. Subtle powers will set the conditions by which you take another step in your healing journey.

(continued)

Begin by identifying a special power you would like to have injected into your heart. That power will help you face your mate with healing words and wisdom. You might wish to draw from the following list:

- Complete faith in a positive outcome!
- The wisdom and knowledge to demonstrate love!
- Words to speak that will dissolve defensiveness!
- The power to project the truth and healing force of your ideas.
- The ability to lovingly and effectively challenge negative beliefs.
- The ability to assimilate, digest and be fueled by love.
- Your own: _____

At the root of everything is love. It is as simple as it sounds. Be faithful, open, and courageous and you will surely make your life different. Before you do the next exercise repeat to yourself the following:

♥ **Heart Prayer:** When love is my focus, my voice is as powerful as I wish it to be.

✎ *Exercise:* ✎
Conversation From the Heart

Go alone to a quiet room, with the intention of being honest with yourself and open to all of your feelings. Bring to mind an emotional hurt or resentment that stems from your relationship with your partner — a hurt that he has never been able to hear without becoming defensive. His lack of acceptance is the main reason this hurt is with you now. The incident may have happened many years ago or as recently as yesterday. Allow yourself to feel all of the emotions related to this hurt.

Imagine your mate sitting in front of you. Begin to tell

him out loud what you are feeling. It is common to feel silly or uncomfortable while doing this type of exercise. Do it anyway and trust your ability to find the deeper meaning in what you feel.

You may want to start the conversation with...

What I have done to myself is...
...given up my own integrity, ignored my wisdom, and allowed my hurt and anger to drown out my deep inner voice.

What I have done to you is...
I have allowed you to think that I am okay. I have covered up my feelings of anger, hurt, and dissatisfaction so you won't know who I really am. I let you think I can handle what has been going on when really, deep down, I can't bear it. I have failed to be honest with you out of fear — fear of your reaction, fear of losing you and of losing us. I have done it for my own survival and that of our family. I have done it because I fear your disapproval and my own feelings of failure.

Talk about every detail, leaving nothing out that is related to this particular incident or issue. Watch for any tendency to invalidate your own feelings, or justify why it happened. For example: "It happened so long ago, and he's changed. I shouldn't still feel this way about what he did." You do a great disservice by not allowing yourself to fully experience your emotions.

When you are finished and have expressed all of your thoughts and feelings, assume his identity in your imagination. Pretend that you are your mate, open-hearted, loving, and totally accepting of you and your feelings. Explain how sorry you are for what took place. Say, "I am so sorry I betrayed you and caused you pain. You never deserved to be treated that way. Please forgive me. I want you to have the peace and security that you need and deserve in your life."

Now, transform yourself into the father figure from your

(continued)

childhood. Be your father standing over you saying exactly the same things. "I'm sorry that you were hurt — you didn't deserve to be treated that way. I want you to forgive me." Wait inside this heart space and see if deeper feelings emerge.

The specific issue always has a deeper origin. Be patient and *want* to know it. It will come. When you know the true genesis of your feelings, you possess the power to transform your relationship. You are capable of speaking about the issue from a different vantage point and are far less threatening to your wounded man. He feels safer and more disposed to discovering his own deeper issues.

If you experience the need to return to and repeat this exercise, don't resist. It can be one of the most exciting journeys you ever take into the far reaches of your powerful heart.

♥ **Heart Prayer:** My partner and I are one, in ways beyond our comprehension. I trust in my longing to heal and grow. The answers emerge when I am ready to know them.

The previous exercise is meant to prepare you to face your partner directly, but first do it to reach new depths of understanding about yourself. The goal for you now is to reach compassion, shedding the tears and mourning the loss so blame does not inhibit the possibility of healing.

These conversations will be possible with him in the future, once your illusions have been shattered. Your truth will then come from the deepest reservoir of your pain. There is never a bottom, only a clear channel to infinite ideas.

Unexpressed pain is more damaging than any other experience of humanness. All of the ideas presented to you thus far are intended to serve as private work. You may feel ready to go into the ring with your partner, but I urge you to be patient and wait until you feel a complete centeredness within you. You will know when the time is right.

You may feel completely skeptical and perhaps frustrated by what you have ahead of you. Please understand that I know how you feel and have spent many of my living hours in confusion, despair and hopelessness. It is enough to want change in your life — to wish for your power back. Things will eventually fall into place. Have compassion for yourself. Be tender to your heart and want to know your greatness. These ideas are steps to lead you there. Have courage and faith that you possess the qualities necessary to change your life script.

The world around you is full of beauty, and so, too, is your inner world. Next, you'll learn how to tap into that infinite reservoir.

It Is Beautiful to Be Fierce

Beauty is a mental atmosphere that is completely opposite the mentality of the beast!

In the fairy tale, the Beast rages, shrieks, and uses his power to subdue the spirits of those around him. He receives attention through his outbursts, using fear tactics to remain in control.

You have experienced this often and know that the beast has power, and uses it against you.

Now that you've met the beast in you — and know the power of the beast in your partner — it is time to own your beauty. Beauty is a far greater force for there are infinite choices in beauty, while the beast is limited by the shadow of dark forces. You can't see when you are in the dark. The love that your beauty offers is a reflection of pleasure and joy. It is free and innocent, grateful and true.

Beauty is a mental atmosphere, not a physical body. Your inner strength, wisdom, and esteem all stem from this illumined core. Your spiritual greatness is born of beauty. It is neither masculine nor feminine, it is a universal vibration that any one of us can tap into. Beauty is your psychic and healing power. Your beauty will tame your beast, and ultimately the beast in your man.

Steps You Take to Heal

1. Accept that you are as much a beast as you are a beauty.
2. Become a beast yourself to understand what she feels like and where she rages and hurts.
3. Go all the way to the bottom of the beast's feelings — to the core, the depths — and discover answers.
   —Once you've opened a path to your beast, leave it open.
   —Attend to the beast on a regular basis.
   —Visualize her fury and fire.
4. Find the beauty that lies in the beast, because this is where the essence of your power exists — where beauty and the beast are one.

Begin to accept your capacity to know love as far greater than you ever imagined. Your beauty is a potent, vital energy helping you to evolve. Release the superficial aspects of beauty and allow the light in your soul to shine outwardly.

Every woman I know longs to utilize her beauty in effective and empowering ways. By using your imagination to realize the dimensions of this never-ending source of strength, your capacity to let in and let out the love you feel will continue to grow. The following are some simple truths about beauty:

- The beauty you seek and long for is always found by reaching into rather than outside yourself.
- Learning to access your beauty costs nothing, yet the rewards are immeasurable.
- Contrary to popular belief, older is not "less-than." You don't have to be young to be beautiful (and you are not necessarily beautiful if you are young).
- You can tap into your beauty right now.

- Reflecting your beauty is easy once you know how to find it.
- Whatever you seek on the outside is available on the inside.
- Your inner beauty is a burning light waiting to greet the world.

By looking into yourself for the keys to your beauty rather than outside for approval from the difficult man in your life (or anyone else), you liberate yourself and, paradoxically, you liberate your relationship.

Beauty Contests

Beauty is in the heart of every one of us, but is often distorted by the superficial influences that surround us. You may be overlooking your deep beauty while comparing yourself to an ideal that you will never be able to live up to, thus locking yourself into a low self-image that impairs your ability to effect change. End the struggle! Understand who you are at the deepest level and use this knowledge as a reference point for how you relate to the rest of the world.

Hidden Beauty

When you resist the idea that you are wounded at your core, you hide much of your natural beauty. However, when you embrace your woundedness, you also embrace deeper dimensions of your natural beauty. There is no need to hide the shadow or the beauty beneath it. You can find that beauty in the dark energy that emanates from the far reaches of your core.

Plastic Beauty

It may seem much easier to rely on outer appearances, yet you live only a shadow of an existence when you put most of your soul's energy into the surface and little or none into the core. You can become very skilled at being the damsel in distress, wondering why only a certain kind of man is attracted to you — the type who is more comfortable focusing on the surface and is unable to embrace the deeper parts of your being, which include your fiery, aggressive, and even angry parts. If you indulge in external modifications while denying yourself the greater challenge and discomfort of internal change, you will fail to achieve the most beautiful results. If external improvements are accompanied with self-improvements, you will get the most from your efforts. Be sure you know you are loved for who you are on the inside before you do any enhancements to the outside.

Aging Beauty

She is the part in each of us who feels one hundred years old — wise in some ways, yet gray and worn through use. A deep psychic pull as powerful as the force of gravity itself is ever-present in our daily lives reminding us of our vulnerability — that life is moving forward and that we are dying. In aging we gain wisdom, thus relieving us of worldly pain. We are meant to surrender, to wither in physical form giving way to nature, eventually becoming one with all. We must surrender and rejoice in the lessons we are forced to learn as we let go. Allow the forces of Mother Nature to unfold you gracefully into your full womanhood.

Inner Beauty

The part of you that glows, that is the bringer of joy, that embraces the sacred feminine heart, is your most alive messenger of love. If you are immersed in sorrow and suffering, this potent side of you is denied. No matter how much you talk about your inner beauty, you never really feel it because all around your heart is a dark energy that projects itself out into the world as suffering. People are aware when they come in contact with you that something is covering up the radiant light that is your inner beauty. If beauty is in the eye of the beholder, then what you see in your innermost world is what you get!

Eternal Beauty

Your eternal beauty is that which creates and destroys. She is the evolutionary spirit of all humankind and holds only love at the core. If you allow the idea of a greater source of strength, far beyond what your imagination can bring into your daily life, you will reap immeasurable rewards. She is the foundation of all that you encounter in your growth process. She is the part of you that manifests the miracles where love is concerned. She is the direct experience of Divine Love. Without her in your life, you will be handicapped. Her guidance will directly affect all aspects of your life.

It is here that you come into contact with your exceptional mind, where daydreams become reality. All the power you hold in loving a wounded man comes from an eternal intuitive mind that envisions all possibilities where love is concerned.

Your capacity to love knows no limits. Your potential in wisdom knows no boundaries. When you place your attention on the idea of eternal beauty and its meaning in your life, your difficulties will be transformed into challenges and opportunities. If you begin to form a relationship with this side of yourself, your mate, upon looking at your face, will also become aware of the eternal beauty. When he looks into your eyes, he will see a deeper, more spirited you. He will recognize your eternal beauty and therein feel safe receiving your love.

If you are willing to accept that these many parts make up

the whole of beauty, you can work on strengthening the aspects of your beauty that are weak. In giving up the struggle to be beautiful, you become more beautiful.

❧ *Exercise:* ❧
Questions About Beauty

- Has your beauty been covered up by toxic feelings such as guilt, anger, hurt, sorrow or shame?
- Is your beauty hidden under fears that you are "not enough?"
- Do you silently agonize over whether to have your body changed surgically?
- Do you know that your beauty is far beyond what you could possibly imagine?
- Are you open to knowing?

♥ **Heart Prayer:** My spirit is my beauty. With courage and determination I can know my beauty and my capacity to effect change in my life. I have the knowledge to weave this timeless thread through all the moments of my days.

Preparing to Change Your Relationship

As women, we are conditioned to doubt ourselves, our strengths, and our beauty. We are also conditioned to ignore the beast in us. We deny our rage, fury and dark energy, robbing ourselves of power to engage comfortably in male-female interactions. However, our greatest resource is our caring heart. When the mirror of the heart is cleansed, we are able to honor and trust this valuable guide. The ability to change conditions that are not working follows naturally. I hope that you are doing the exercises in this book. They will help you to reconnect with the center of loving power deep within your soul, and they will give you the tools to release the hurt, anger, shame, and guilt that may currently surround your heart.

With an unburdened heart, you position yourself to decide what your needs and wishes really are, and what changes you want in your relationship. By allowing the beast that wounds you (your internal beast) to become the beauty that heals you, you transform yourself.

In a later chapter, you will learn how to reach your healing power — the place where change occurs. Sometimes you will cross by yourself, other times, he will go with you. Gradually, as you share with him assurances of your love, he will experience the joy of receiving the love that surrounds him. Though he may recoil at first, remain steadfast and gradually share with him the most transforming power on earth.

Keep your goals modest; take one step at a time. Healing and growth in the relationship cannot occur all at once. The initial objective is to change the current shape of the relationship, bringing together two individuals who have been drifting apart so that they may once again grow together.

One critical ingredient that often gets lost in long-term relationships is magic. The only real miracles occur through love, and you have the power to create them. That power is your birthright, your gift! The first step is to become connected (or reconnected) to your own source of loving power. The next step is to deeply understand yourself and your relationship to the wounded male you brought into your life. If he resists change, it may be because of something you are resisting. Finally, you must apply your new wisdom to heal specific problems in your relationship.

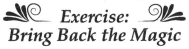

Exercise:
Bring Back the Magic

In preparing for a change, explore an important dimension of freedom. Realize that a new seed has been planted in you and, in order for that seed to grow, accept that you have

(continued)

the power to create magic.
- Know that you want it.
- Go after it as if your life is at stake — because your aliveness is.
- Dare to reach beyond and take one chance.
- Write a note in your appointment book: "The magic I am creating is ..." Keep writing it down until it happens.

♥ **Heart Prayer:** I use my dynamic energy to expect magic. I can manifest change by simply expecting it! I deserve it!

5
Developing Emotional Literacy

However unpleasant a feeling may be,
it is useful and "proper"
given the context in which it occurs.
It can call attention to something that needs to be done ...
Solutions to many of life's problems
come not from struggling with them,
but from merging with them, adapting to them,
accepting them for what they are.
—David Reynolds, Ph.D.,
A Handbook for Constructive Living

With few exceptions, what many of us call negative emotions — the anger, despair, loneliness, jealousy, envy, guilt and shame that surface when we embrace our inner beast — are not in themselves negative. Negative outcomes occur only when we direct the emotional energy of these feelings in destructive ways — against ourselves or our love partners.

All emotions hold a valuable place in our day-to-day awareness and growth. Emotional literacy is the ability to recognize, understand and appropriately express feelings. Becoming emotionally literate helps us initiate and respond honestly and effectively when dealing with a wounded partner. Communicating from a firm emotional base confers clarity and integrity in our encounters. Surprisingly, the ability to appropriately feel and express anger and other dark emotions is one of the richest aspects of emotional literacy.

Anger is the feeling through which you declare your rights, boundaries and innermost values to yourself and the world. When you listen to your own anger (focused anger, not just weariness and irritation at things in general) and express it appropriately, you show where you stand, and make change possible.

"In a broad sense, to have and express any emotion, negative or positive, presupposes that one cares, that one is engaged, that one has interests, that one takes something personally," writes Dr. Robert C. Solomon in *About Love: Reinventing Romance.* "No one, not even a saint, can have a sense of justice without the capacity for anger and outrage, even the ability to hate. Indeed, one might well argue that justice is impossible without hatred, or at least without the hatred of evil and outrage at the sight of injustice. The heart of justice may be compassion for others, but its origins and its passions are to be found in the more violent, even hostile emotions. Mercy, grace, and forgiveness may...be important civil and religious virtues, but they presuppose, rather than merely oppose, such vehement emotions as vengeance. Our sense of justice may dream about and aim at peace and universal contentment, but it is also bound to give due weight to our competitiveness, our acquisitiveness, and our 'rights'."

In the days and weeks ahead, make it a point to begin perceiving so-called "negative" or "bad" emotions in a different way. Acknowledge that these feelings arise in your heart through the wisdom of your inner beast and for reasons that are important to you and your love partner. Rather than denying or repressing them, respond in constructive and healthful ways.

Stop Denying Your Feelings

The typical first response is to avoid or resist unpleasant emotions. Yet growing evidence suggests that darker emotions are highly useful signals that things you care about are at risk. Rather than push these emotions away, allow yourself to feel them. Invite them to guide you to the lair of your inner beast. Fully experiencing unpleasant emotions is the fastest way through them, the most efficient way to direct the energy that they create. According to the research of Daniel Wegner, Ph.D., Professor of Psychology at Trinity University in San Antonio and author of *White Bears and Other Unwanted Thoughts,* if you attempt to deny or suppress dark thoughts or feelings, they inevitably loom larger and longer. By acknowledging a distressing thought or feeling, allowing yourself to feel or think it, you take away much of its power to control you and to produce hurtful or destructive behavior toward you or your mate. Feelings which are denied find innumerable insidious ways to surface in your life.

Anger can be a remarkable catalyst for creative alternative thinking. Anger has elicited moral courage and fueled revolutions that lead to greater justice in social institutions. If you are seeking a revolution in your relationship, let anger serve as your drummer.

Many great books have been written and works of art created to escape sadness or loss. A dose of fear or anxiety serves a useful purpose so long as it is controlled. Worry prompts us to rehearse for dangerous encounters with our mate, and a small jolt of fretfulness can help focus the mind on problems in our relationship and aid in the search for solutions. Pitfalls don't appear until worrying blocks reasoning or crowds out perseverance with resignation. Over-worrying about failing increases the likelihood of failure.

Justice, often the result of constructive discontent, cannot be based on pure rationality. Emotions make up the very core of virtually all appeals for justice. Emotions like outrage, resentment and vengeance arise when we sense that we are being cheated or deprived in our relationship, or when we experience the need for fairness and responsibility from our mate.

A hallmark of emotional literacy is the ability to acknowledge dark feelings instead of denying them, and to recognize the signs of discontent early, dealing with them honestly and turning them into something of value. During the early moments of a dark emotion, allow its energy to move you. Remember, by definition, emotion means "movement of spirit": movement from what is wrong to what is right, to what matters, to the path of growth and, ultimately, healing. As Swiss psychologist C.G. Jung explained, "There is no light without shadow and no wholeness without imperfection."

✂ *Exercise:* ✂
Dark Emotions

Look deeply and consider the following questions:
- What darker emotions are you aware of in your own life? Do these dark feelings remind you of any past loss or betrayal? What is the first memory you have of anger? Rage? Resentment? Are you comfortable acknowledging and expressing your dark feelings? Do these feelings prompt you to get defensive or give up?
- What is the worst thing you've ever done in terms of failing or betraying another person? What darker emotions came up? How did you face them and keep going? What happened then? What did you learn from this?
- What, right now, is your greatest fear about the future of your love relationship?
- Beneath the fear, what is the truth or apparent deeper truth about this situation? Can you face it, and if so, how?
- If you were to do what is really deep in your heart, with

whom or what would you be in conflict?
- What are the two most important problems or issues in your relationship that you have avoided facing?
- What are the deeper fears that are keeping you from reaching specific goals?
- If you knew that these fears would always be present, would you be willing to feel the fear and move ahead anyway in the direction of your goals?
- About what, specifically, do you feel envy, jealousy or malice? Can you feel these dark emotions as energy rather than condemnations of your own capabilities or present situation? Is there someone at whom you can look and constructively say, "She is doing this really well. Why can't I, as well?" using the discomforting energy of jealousy, envy or malice?

♥ **Heart Prayer:** When I open the doors of darkness that lie within me, my fears are released and a new day dawns.

Emotional Growth

One of the things I've come to appreciate is that emotional literacy is not about perfectionism. As we work to improve ourselves, our relationships and the world around us, our emotions help show us how, when and where to take action. But if we begin to think that we must make everything perfect, we become anxious, tense, frustrated, even frantic, easily unbalanced by emotions or circumstances. Setbacks occur, triggering worry and despair.

It can be incredibly liberating to give up perfectionism. Often it is the expectation of perfection ("I shouldn't have let this happen; I should have said/not said/felt/done this...") that undermines us, especially when situations are beyond our control. Nevertheless, we feel defeated or inadequate, feelings that are legitimate unless they result from an imposed standard of perfectionism. We do our best, especially when faced with a difficult and emotionally challenging relationship.

As Emerson observed, "Emotional balance is just as vital as mental and physical balance, and requires treating yourself with respect, forgiving your mistakes, accepting many of your stumbles and inadequacies in life while holding in mind and heart the purpose and vision of where you are headed, no matter how long it takes along the way."

When Impressionist painter Claude Monet speaks of "working hard, feeling my way," I believe he is speaking about the value of emotional resilience. Many dimensions of emotional literacy are wedded to the development of resilience: creativity; faith; the ability to face, tolerate and transcend pain; independence of spirit; the ability to restore self-respect and self-esteem when they are diminished or temporarily lost; and a capacity for learning; the ability to ask for support and to continue to love during difficult times.

Dimensions of Emotional Healing

Emotional healing is the healthy, transformational release that occurs when you make peace with your heart's innermost burdens and wounds. It is a healing process that is linked through the immune system to every part of the body and mind. Above all else, emotional healing is an act of love and forgiveness. Whatever our wounds — a sense of fear or shame, the shadows of guilt or rage, bitter disappointment in our love relationship, the sacrifice of a job or a home, or any of life's thousands of emotional hurts — emotional healing is an opportunity for growth and illumination, for newfound pride in our resilience and faith.

When emotional healing occurs, a deep sense of liberation and of spiritual awakening follows. We feel whole inside and trust more deeply in life's wisdom and the voice of the heart.

"Excessive holding back of thoughts and feelings can place people at risk for both major and minor diseases," says psychologist and educator James W. Pennebaker.

Every time we face a long-suppressed emotional burden or a new painful limitation, we are given the chance to move through it. When we make peace with the pain, we transform it into a radiant source of renewal and become healthier and stronger because of it.

You might be wondering, "How do I know I have suppressed emotions? I don't feel burdened by anything right now." You may not be aware that suppressed emotions constrict your ability to love, but it always begins with you.

Grief Spares No One

It's a universal truth: Sometimes life seems to fall apart. Grief spares no one. It can strike suddenly, grip your heart like a vise, and its emotional pain can last for months, even years. Yet traumatic experiences are also life's turning points.

Whenever you are faced with a severe crisis, your mind and heart are inundated with feelings of helplessness and defeat. You are pressed into a desperate search for hope — an effort to make sense of your life. If left unresolved, these traumatic experiences may suppress the body's immune system and leave you more vulnerable to illness or disease.

Think back to the most traumatic moment in your relationship. Do you remember feeling helpless, hurt or furious? Do you recall asking, "Why me? What did I do to deserve this? Will my life ever be normal again? I wish I could stop the world from turning right now! How can I handle this?" In *Primitive Mythology: The Masks of God,* Joseph Campbell shares an ancient Eskimo maxim: "The only true wisdom lies far from Mankind, out in the great loneliness, and it can be reached only through suffering. Privation and suffering alone can open the mind of a man to all that is hidden to others."

No matter how healthy you are, grief from severe change or loss can cause profound distress, among the most painful of life's experiences. But difficult as it is, grieving can't be avoided or hurried. Grieving is a natural healing process that takes time and patience. The grief I experienced when confronted with my husband's infidelity ran a long and tortuous route through my emotions — sadness, hopelessness, fear, anxiety, sleeplessness, confusion and agonized crying. Grief can also lead to loss of appetite, preoccupation with objects and locations associated with the loss, and dreams of the people and incidents involved. Yet all of these emotions and thoughts are normal healthy responses. It's important to recognize this, since doubts about your ability to cope can lead to depression.

Perhaps more than anything else, grieving signifies how deeply we cared about that which is lost. The thing to do is live from one moment to the next, accepting all of the confusing and dark feelings that arise. Be patient with yourself and give the emotions associated with grief permission to surface, be experienced and then released.

Emotional Healing Through Private Journaling

Growing evidence from studies involving thousands of people of all ages and backgrounds suggests that a significant emotional healing effect can come from spending as little as five to fifteen minutes a day, for several days, writing in a private journal about whatever issues and experiences are getting you down.

The process of emotion-centered writing can help you to better acknowledge and understand deep emotions that need healing and release. You must really let go and trust that what is expressed from your heart can help heal the hurts of the past and remove barriers in your life. The benefits of writing come from expressing the deepest thoughts and feelings surrounding personal upheavals and traumas from the recent or distant past.

Set aside fifteen to twenty minutes a day for several days to write down your deepest thoughts and feelings surrounding disturbing issues. You will gain new understanding and insight and, at the same time, foster better physical health. A similar benefit can come from talking honestly with a trusted friend, outside of your relationship.

Start at the beginning of your "personal story" — whatever it is that you feel strongly about and want to work through or heal. Let the feelings unfold from the start of the experience and allow your heart to guide you. Try not to edit or make corrections as you write — let your feelings flow without censorship. Express the truth of the way you feel it now.

Journaling Guidelines

1. Allow yourself to give up control, to let go and free your feelings to flow naturally and truthfully.
2. Trust that what you express is your own emotional truth.
3. Let go of the need to justify why you feel a certain way or to explain things from another person's perspective. Give yourself full permission to explore the depths of your feelings.
4. Do not anticipate showing your journal to your partner, since this would impede the natural flow of your feelings while writing. Also, sharing the journal could do more harm than good while you are working things out.

While writing, focus on the issues that you are currently living with, and explore both the objective experience (what happened) and your feelings about it. Write about your deepest emotions — what you feel about the issues and why. Don't be concerned if you temporarily feel worse. You may feel sad or somewhat depressed during or after writing. This is normal. After all, you are uncovering difficult feelings and holding them in your awareness. Most negative feelings fade within an hour or so. In rare cases, they may last a day or two. The overwhelming majority of people studied have reported feelings of relief, happiness, and contentment soon after an emotional journaling session is concluded. Another benefit of emotional journaling is that you can look back over a few months' or years' worth of writing and see just how much you have grown and learned.

Journaling is a tool for emotional literacy that allows even your deepest, darkest feelings to come "straight from the heart." Ideally, we should all be able to express our most intimate thoughts to another person. This kind of sharing can forge a powerful and lasting bond with others, and offers both physiological and psychological health benefits. However, sharing is risky. If you unburden yourself and are then rejected by the listener, you may become hostile, depressed, or withdrawn. What matters most is that your feelings need to be felt and expressed safely, in this case through private journaling. Some people have truly hurt others by confiding their feelings. Although they claim to be open and honest in their actions, their disclosures are clearly motivated by revenge. Be aware of your motivation if you are considering opening up communication.

Emotional Sex

We all seek intimacy and passion, sensing that these conditions would be truly wonderful if only we could attain and sustain them. What we fail to realize is that intimate love is not some vague goal, but is in fact the natural and highest expression of an emotional atmosphere of trust and passion created by two loving partners. The result — intimate, resonant love — is the most celebrated of emotional unions. Yet it is largely a mystery, looked for and longed for but rarely found.

Look inside your heart. How do you define love? It is my contention that love is a purely emotional process that takes time and care. Through emotional openness, love's pleasures and pains can be experienced and its richness celebrated. If we think of ourselves as having multiple layers of emotion, then the deepest form of intimacy and love requires the unwrapping of these layers until at last we are able to stand in each other's presence with the secrets of our innermost hearts revealed.

To a great extent, the way you love determines the way you live.

Love is based, first of all, on caring for your own emotional well-being. At the same time, it requires that you care for your mate as you care for yourself. If you can come to better understand what love is and refuse to suffocate it or take it for granted, then love becomes an invigorating force that reaches into the future and sets a foundation for trust and excitement, for wholehearted sharing, for impassioned, meaningful living. Loving relationships are built, not found. They depend on a foundation of safety and trust and have little if anything to do with luck. And, contrary to popular opinion, they have absolutely nothing to do with "being made for each other."

✎❧ *Exercise:* ❦✎
Blocks to Love.

Take out a piece of paper and complete the following:
- Sometimes I hold back my passion in love because...
- I want to feel valued and cherished by my partner but sometimes I feel blocked by...
- The reason I feel this is...

♥ **Heart Prayer:** All the intimacy I am looking for on the outside will come to me when I am willing to explore the depths of feeling I have on the inside.

Love is nothing less than the creation — or re-creation — of one's most personal identity. And the core, or essence, of love is the realization that you *are* what you love; you *are* what you care about. "Only someone who is ready for everything, who doesn't exclude any experience, even the most incomprehensible, will live the relationship with another person as something alive and will himself sound the depths of his own being," wrote the poet Rainer Maria Rilke. "For if we imagine this being of the individual as a larger or smaller room, it is obvious that most people come to know only one corner of their room, one spot near the window, one narrow strip on which they keep walking back and forth."

When sex is great, it is easily taken for granted; but when it is bad it can consume the consciousness of a relationship. Unfulfilling sex is often the result of a lack of openness and honesty in the relationship. When two people hold back their feelings, they inevitably hold back sexually. It is ironic that one of life's most exceptional pleasures is fraught with so many hidden obstacles. Among the most insidious of these impediments are the aging-sex stereotypes, which tell us that sex is no longer great or frequent by age thirty-five, forty-five, sixty or beyond.

These myths persist despite recent studies showing some couples in their nineties enjoying sex two or three times a week. Trapped by misconceptions, few of us ever come close to realizing our lifelong potential for sexual energy. Sexual energy is directly linked to emotional energy, to passion. The more we feel, the more our sexual vitality emerges. It is the most natural "turn on."

Great sex is not something that just happens; it comes no more automatically than great adult conversation. It has to be learned — in a shared, sensitive, openly emotional or passionate atmosphere. What's emerging from scientific studies is a whole new model of human sexuality — one that emphasizes pleasure, closeness, and self- and partner-enhancement rather than "performance." Few of life's experiences yield greater rewards, since as our intimate relationships become more vibrant and aware, so in turn do we.

The energy of sexual desire resides, and is nourished or confounded, in the emotions.

Deep intimacy and emotionally extraordinary sex depend at all times on a genuine sense of safety and trust. This requires that you and your partner be emotionally honest and clear with each other every time you are making sensual or sexual contact — not just in body but in your minds and shared words. You must tell each other what pleases and what displeases or hurts. Research indicates that extraordinary "super sex" is only possible when both partners feel completely safe, when they trust in letting go and open themselves emotionally to deepening pleasures above and beyond orgasm. This requires listening to the voice of your own heart and your partner's heart. If ongoing, unresolved emotionally-charged issues exist between you and your partner, journaling may help you open up and free you to be in the moment during sex. Often, we are not fully aware of how we feel, or why. We must find appropriate ways to acknowledge, express and learn

from a wide range of emotions in ourselves and our love partner, which will free us from the urge to punish or control our
partners through sexual withholding or emotional withdrawal
during sex.

You can create this type of deep emotional and sexual intimacy consciously, through openness, intention and practice.
Commit to unveiling old emotional blockages, changing and
moving beyond them. In time your partner will open up and
heal emotional wounds as well and the sexual bonds between
the two of you will deepen.

✒ *Exercise:* ✒
Sensory Body Tour

To develop exceptional skill in sensual and emotionally-
responsive sexual touch, this is one of the most effective exercises.

Choose a quiet, private room and select a lighting level
(bright, dim, or dark) that is pleasing both to you and your
partner. If a certain aroma arouses you (and is also enjoyed
by your partner), create a hint of that scent in the room. If
you both enjoy soft background music, put some on. Take
the phone off the hook, put your favorite sheets on the bed,
and do whatever else you both wish to "set the scene" in a
most enjoyable way.

Wearing as little or as much as you like, guide your
partner's hands with your own on a special tour of every
square inch of your body, showing him exactly how you like
to be touched. Move in response to whatever touches you
find most erotic, most stimulating and desirable. If you or
your partner enjoy whispered love messages, then be certain they are given and received, but don't rely on words
and sound sensations alone to create erotic passion. Once
you have covered every part of your body, switch roles and
let your lover guide you.

"The feeling of touch, and the emotional responses it raises, can be difficult to discuss with words," says Linda Perlin Alperstein, Ph.D. "What does it mean if I tell you I like 'light' or 'medium' touch? That can mean different things to different people. It's much easier to demonstrate. Let your fingers do the talking. Of course, you can talk while conducting a Body Tour, but simple 'oohs' and 'ahhhs' can be just as communicative as words. If you feel ill at ease naming certain parts of the body, the Body Tour allows you to show your partner how you like to be touched there without saying anything."

Some ancient Asian philosophers and physicians believed that exquisitely sensual, masterfully controlled sex replenished and strengthened the life force, or energy, of both men and women. The prevailing idea was that sexual vitality and potency depended, first and foremost, on emotional and sensory awareness and sensual expertise.

If men were to listen to private conversations among women, they would likely hear that, "The best foreplay for me is when he listens to my feelings and encourages me to open my heart all the way before we make love. I get so turned on by that!" If women were to listen to private conversations among men, they would likely hear the complaint that, "Women withhold themselves and are so unresponsive during sex." An important reason for the lack of enthusiasm many women feel is the fact that they tend to become aroused more slowly than men, and want an intimate emotional connection; when a man rushes lovemaking it turns his partner off.

To enjoy emotionally resonant sex, it is essential to suspend judgment long enough to approach lovemaking in fresh, original, highly sensitive ways. It's helpful to get out of ruts and routines as soon as they become so comfortable that your, or your partner's, sense of passion vanishes. Researchers have found, for example, that "super-sexual women" have learned to approach each moment with an openness to feelings and new emotional experiences referred to as a "beginner's mind" — approaching each sexual interlude as if it were the first.

This simply requires practice. Don't jump ahead with your thoughts. Instead, just keep pace with the wonderful information you receive through your senses. Follow whatever erotic thoughts emerge, responding spontaneously and naturally to your partner's body, touch and voice without "analyzing." Teach your mind to follow your fingertips and hands in discovering new sensations. Recreate the image you had when you first kissed your partner's lips passionately. Let your senses lead your mind. Let the energy of your emotions direct your sensations and guide you into a more beautiful and satisfying sexual experience.

Sexual energy increases for many of us when we feel free to relate how we are feeling right now, in the changing, evolving experience of intimacy, and have our partner do the same. By describing sensations of closeness, we heighten feelings of sensuality. By using warm, emotionally explicit dialogue, complimenting how the other person looks and feels and expressing our own sensations of arousal and pleasure, we can more easily distance ourselves from unwanted thoughts and begin to share our deepest feelings. For example, "That touch or word feels nurturing to me" or "I feel closest to you when you wrap your arms around me and hold me for a few minutes." Using the word *feel* establishes an openness and caring that helps automatically to draw you closer together.

✂ Exercise: ✂
Borrowing From Past Experiences
Write a detailed description of an emotionally fulfilling sexual experience — one that you actually experienced in the past or one that you wish to experience in the future.

Use all of your senses and explore every layer of feeling leading up to the peak of ecstasy and beyond. What felt best? Where? When? Bring your emotions, mind, body, and soul together into the experience. You deserve to feel passion and aliveness through developing and exploring a fulfilling sexual relationship. Listen to the voice of your heart: What does it say and need? Which elements of this passionate intimacy do you want to carry with you in your heart and senses during future interactions with your partner?

♥ **Heart Prayer:** I deserve sexual intimacy with emotional closeness. New discoveries of passionate pleasure await me.

✂ *Exercise:* ✂
Heart-Centered Dialogue

Heart-centered dialogue is the active, constructive use of your heart's energy, and it will lead you to resolution of the problems and difficulties in your life. It is, at its very core, a reflection of the deeper intention of your heart. Here are several guidelines for effective heart-centered dialogue:

1. *What* is my true intention in expressing this emotional energy? To inform honestly? To release a burden? To learn or clarify something? To create more openness and understanding? To express caring or love? To build rapport or trust? To forgive?
2. *What*, specifically, do I want to communicate? Should I communicate with words or without? How will I know that my true meaning is heard by the other person?
3. *When* is my message best heard? Do I really need to say this now?
4. *Where* is my message best heard?
5. *How* can I communicate in the most honest, caring, and personally effective way?

(continued)

Emotional energy can be guided in a number of other ways. One of the most useful is to clearly ask for what you want or need. This is such a simple yet profound approach, and few of us actually do it. Instead, we talk in circles, we ask leading questions, we hint, we hope, we expect, we fume when no one seems to notice. We resort to tactics such as pouting, whining, manipulation, withdrawal, sarcasm, or back-stabbing. Instead, ask!

Asking for what you need or want reveals your true humanity, your open heart. Yes, at times you may be hurt or rejected, but less often than you anticipate. The more you ask, the more the odds increase that you will get your needs met.

All too often we think that if other people really care about us, or love us, we won't have to ask for what we want or need— they will automatically know! Rarely, however, is this true, even though with emotional literacy it is easier to sense what others are feeling. Mistakes will still be made unless we ask for clarification. There are two core parts to a heart-centered dialogue:

1. This is what I *experienced* and *felt*.

2. This is what I *want* or *need*.

In some situations, the best way to guide emotional energy is through silent actions-from-the-heart. For example, say nothing negative to yourself or the other person. Instead, simply change the focus of your attention. Use your emotional energy to fuel a few minutes of creative thinking, to take a brief walk or engage in some other form of exercise, or to find a quiet space for some personal learning, healing, planning or reflection.

♥ **Heart Prayer:** Though I am terrified by the vulnerability I feel at risking the truth, I will take the journey deep into my heart.

Resolve Daily Conflicts Through Feeling

To be able to state your feelings to a partner ("My feelings are hurt by what you just said to me. Did you really mean...?") or to read his feeling and try to clarify what you sense ("Have I offended you in some way? I can tell you pulled away. Are you upset with me?") is emotional literacy at work. To get to this place where you are actively guiding the energy of emotions, open your heart and ask the **FEEL-LISTEN-GUIDE** questions:

1. Which deep emotion is getting my attention right now? **(FEEL)**
2. What is the wake-up message I am receiving? **(LISTEN)**
3. How can I best guide this emotional energy? **(GUIDE)**

Ask one question at a time, and have the courage to be honest with yourself about what you feel. Go deeper, speak up, clarify what your body and senses are telling you, and move toward more authentic communication with others. Sometimes this means saying no to requests, or clarifying what you sense is a put-down or put-off. You may find out that it's not what you thought it was. Being direct — appropriately expressing your anger or other feelings — allows you to honor both yourself and the person who did something, or appeared to do something, that offended or distressed you. You honor yourself by revealing the limits of what you will tolerate. You honor the other person by inviting him or her to become more aware of the effects of his or her words and behaviors. And once you release the uncomfortable feelings of confusion or anger inside you, the negative spin of this energy is shortened. A more caring part of your heart is revealed. Suddenly, you are spending less time on needless emotional recovery work that results from misperceiving the feelings of others.

✒ Exercise: ✒
Guiding Your Emotional Energy

Take out a piece of paper or a blank journal and record some of the ways you might begin to guide your emotional energy into greater self-discovery.

Trust: Write down all of the ways in which you might be mistrusting the intentions or feelings of yourself or others. List specific steps that you can take to become more open and trusting of other people and of your own deeper self.

Healing: There is always need of healing, often beginning with yourself. Note places where your heart tells you it has suffered from rejection or denial. How can you accept these hurts and fill the empty aches with new love and light instead?

Kindness, empathy, compassion: These loving qualities are expressions of your inherent and conscious goodness. They put your caring intentions into action. Make a list of the people to whom you wish to exude these heart qualities in the days ahead.

Perseverance or commitment: Pick one emotional block, such as anger, jealousy, shame, or resentment, and commit yourself to shaking off its lingering burden.

Inner strength: If you treat your feelings as fragile, they will be. Instead, practice favoring your strength and resilience, recalling times in the past when you have prevailed in the face of loss or uncertainty. Name one specific area of your life and relationships where you wish to become stronger. Commit to using emotional literacy skills in that area.

Love: List the specific ways you experience feeling loved by people with whom you have relationships: parents, children, a love partner, friends. How might you open your heart to giving and receiving greater love?

Seven Simple Steps to Greater Emotional Literacy with Your Mate

So many women have asked me about ways to begin nurturing emotional literacy in partnerships that I have created seven basic guideposts.

1. Above all else, respect and value your mate from the heart and with your love.
2. Recognize your mate's need to open up and share his feelings at the right time and in the right way for him.
3. Be aware that your own presence can help create an atmosphere of safety and trust. Be empathetic, patient, loving, open and forgiving.
4. Allow all feelings and thoughts, yours and his, to be shared without interruption or explanation. This actively demonstrates how much you value your mate as a unique and worthy person.
5. Accept your mate's feelings without judgment. Remain interested and even curious, and don't defend yourself or your positions. Acknowledge your mate for having the courage to tell you how he feels.
6. If appropriate, say, "I'm sorry that you have been hurt and have had a difficult time" or "I'm sorry for my part in hurting you."
7. Help your mate come to his own conclusions. If he asks your advice, give it; otherwise, just listen and ask emotionally literate questions to help him in his own discovery process.

Give your mate a chance to give to you. All you need to do is open your heart to those moments in which he offers you love, love in any form — his form. Be ready to read love in a touch, a look, a kind word, a simple action, a gesture, a smile. Allow yourself to receive it.

6

Unlocking Your Healing Power

Healing winds continue to blow
And soon will reach their goal
Though barriers many have blocked the way
Its mission will be won.
— Adele Tinning

Somewhere within you is the power to change things — to heal the unhealthy parts of your life, putting an end once and for all to cycles of failure and defeat. The legacy that has been passed on to you, that you will leave to your daughters and all the daughters of the earth, can only change when you take action in your daily life — when you become a woman who uses her healing power, is mature and wise, stands up for what she believes, communicates openly and freely, and continues to find deeper ways to love and connect with those around her. The woman you must become is instinctually drawn to find meaning and purpose in each day's experiences. She is restricted only by the limits she places on her life.

Developing Spiritual Esteem

A person with spiritual esteem is one who listens to her innermost wisdom and acts according to the laws of love and right action. She knows the true value of love and puts this above all other values. When well endowed with spiritual esteem, she directs her passion and power toward life-affirming, positive and enriching experiences, no matter where she is or whom she is with. She is grounded in spirit as well as graceful on the physical plane. The woman with spiritual esteem is able to transcend her personal self and connect with her higher self.

In my experience, a woman with spiritual esteem possesses these qualities:
- Active in healing and growth
- Believes in inner guidance and intuition
- Empties the pain to allow the pleasure
- Takes time to meditate, relax and be with God
- Reaches for answers in spiritual awareness
- Enjoys ritual
- Dreams of beauty and grace
- Walks in nature and lets it in
- Celebrates life

If you are constrained and constricted by an unhealthy love relationship, you have failed to realize — yet probably hunger to know — that you possess immeasurable healing capabilities. Beyond the task of simply raising your self-esteem lies a whole new realm — the realm where your *real* power lives. Developing your spiritual esteem will further your evolutionary process, transform the example you present to the young women in your life and lay a new foundation, for all time, under your life script. Your most potent gift is the part of you that gives birth to new life, above and beyond the physical realm. You can point the way — away from dark and negative forces that confine you and your family — toward a new, un-explored realm.

Your ability to forgive, accept, trust and be patient is dependent upon how often you use your spiritual esteem.

Female Energy Can Heal Male Wounds

In a primitive sense, women have a strong physical and emotional attachment to the family unit. This communion can create a stable foundation beneath the weaker structure of the male personality. You must believe in your stabilizing abilities and know that comfortable coexistence can only be realized through your willingness to reinvent yourself and determine in a unique way what is fair and just. You gain dignity and become an example to him by focusing on your own spiritual esteem.

If you lose yourself and operate in a survival mode, you cannot hope to facilitate change in your partner. You are simply tuning into his insecurities and reinforcing them. On the other hand, if you courageously engage him in learning the pleasures of talking truth, and are willing to be an instrument for the growth of your life together, the miracles of love will prevail.

You have a biological understanding of what it really means to be loved. By knowing the hunger in your wounded man for connectedness, acceptance, adoration, and safety — a blend of conditions that may have been largely lacking in his life — you have a powerful effect on the growth of the relationship.

You must drop out of any competitive games with him and stand inside your most creative feminine self, re-imagining love and compassion as often as you possibly can. This will allow your instinctual qualities to assume their most effective role.

If your goal is to get him to conform to your wishes so you can feel safe, then you are the one controlling the relationship and ultimately you postpone the lessons necessary for its advancement. However, when you turn your attention to your strengths and to actualizing your healing potential, change occurs instantly. Too often, women focus on the negative (even in their thoughts) and reinforce negative behavior rather than paying attention to positive qualities and reinforcing the good. By giving up control of what he does and how he does it, you give your relationship an opportunity to reach a new level of love.

Building the basic belief that you can effect change will cause a shift and lead you closer to a satisfying life with your partner. You can be any character you wish. If you step into the role of Beauty, adding the power of love to your daily existence, you combine your growth as an individual with your powers as a woman, creating real and lasting change.

Aspiring to possess a divine personality gives you infinite choices in helping the relationship to its full potential. Reaching inward for answers and utilizing the knowledge in your daily life helps you have choices. No other being is like you. You have your own eternal destiny to follow. Reaching for self-realization along the way gives you the focused energy to bring about change in your life. When you identify what you need to know about yourself, you are able to assess the burning issues in your relationship. The following exercise will begin the process. Keep in mind that your feminine nature is powerful and holds infinite secrets to unlocking your love and healing power.

✎ *Exercise:* ✎
Removing Blocks of Powerlessness

Follow these steps:

1. Wake yourself up from your deep sleep. Pinch yourself. Do anything you can to help you open your eyes to the truth of how powerless you feel.
2. Identify one situation that blocks you from loving yourself and then loving him.
3. Acknowledge what you do to yourself and to him when it happens.
4. Prepare yourself to change the situation by letting the old images die off. See them in your mind's eye, withering away. Grieve over them. Let them go.
5. Notice the empty space that appears.
6. Now write down the extreme opposite of the situation you identified in (2).

For example, change this...

Every time my partner gets angry with me, his face changes, becoming tight and tense. I feel rejected in that moment and my love is blocked.

...to this:

Every time my partner gets angry with me, I let his harsh looks and words pass through me. I feel strong and my love for him is undiminished.

The next time you feel your flow of love blocked, try using this healing technique on yourself, doing the opposite of what you would normally do. Don't waste one more day of your life being stuck. See yourself open and free from the constraints of reactive behavior. Oppose your old position. You will be amazed at the incredible change, not just in you, but in him. When his negative actions are consistently met with your positive nature, he will eventually see no payoff to remaining stuck.

♥ **Heart Prayer:** The burden of "what's wrong" is replaced with "what's right." I move out of the darkness into the light.

Healing Tools

You cannot fulfill your healing potential without proper healing tools. Infinite choices are available to you. Healing power tools will help trigger the compassionate energy you need. The results will be rewarding, and you will be making efficient use of your time and energy to promote an atmosphere of change. But first some basic areas of your personality may need to be strengthened.

Habitual failure stems from inertia, locked-in energy with nowhere to go. By unlocking and directing your healing energy, you will break unhealthy patterns that plague your life. True fulfillment stems from pulling yourself up away from defeat and reaching for new concepts that will work in your daily life.

You Are a Healer

Through the ages women have been the greatest healers, by giving birth, helping others through the life-death cycle, bathing the new life as well as the old. The ritual of cultivating healing herbs in ancient times was no different than your rushing to the health-foods store to buy healing remedies for your family. Healing is deeply rooted in your personality and is part of your heritage.

Many women are instilled with life-giving devotion which accords to those closest to them a powerful feeling of belonging. As healers, these women are inventive and assiduous in improving the quality of life around them. It is the wonderful quality of feminine intuition that grants women keener senses, more acute powers of observation, analytical adeptness and better memory. These skills were developed in females to ensure the survival of the young. Consider how useful these rich qualities will be in healing yourself and, ultimately, your relationship.

Acknowledge the fact that you possess healing power. What you believe to be true becomes true! What you place attention on grows stronger. You are a healer. Cultivate the immense storehouse of creativity that will allow your life to blossom.

Give Up Martyrdom — It's Boring!

A necessary pre-condition to bringing out the healer in you is to make sure you are not dragging your martyr-self into this process. If you are, it simply won't work.

The martyr is the part of you that thinks and acts based on self-pity, guilt, anger and hostility or hurt. This part of you wants to heal your relationship because you see no alternative.

Nancy said to me in counseling, "Sure, I'll try to heal my marriage — he certainly won't do anything about it. I guess it's my job."

I quickly responded, "You are doing this for the wrong reason. I'm not saying that you are wrong in your assessment of the relationship. You *are* leading the way, but do it because of what you'll gain from the experience in the way of growth for yourself. If you stay where you are, you'll be accepting your smallness, rather than discovering your greatness. What a gift! If you drop the familiar mind-tapes the martyr plays inside your head, you will discover uncharted territory and feel a sense of magic and mystery about your life!"

The Paradox

To accomplish a healing goal it is imperative that you accept a potentially disturbing paradox about your own nature: *You are as dark as you are light.* You are as much beast as you are beauty. Before you look to heal something in your relationship, look at the dark force within you. Peer into the creases of your own personality to see how and why this is a problem in your life. If you don't know, simply be willing to know. The questions that live inside can't be answered until they are asked. Call upon a higher guide to help you discover these truths. If any ideas come to you, hold them loosely in your awareness. Soon, subtle pieces of information will begin to float across your mental screen.

Extending the paradox even further: Be terribly committed to your healing plan, yet unattached to the outcome. I know this is asking a lot, but if you can do it, the journey will be more enjoyable and satisfying.

Trust Yourself

Trusting something with which you lack familiarity can be very difficult. In the process of claiming your healing power, you'll become acutely aware of certain blind spots. Don't be alarmed. There is always a gap between learning and knowing. If you trust in your true nature and have compassion for yourself along the way, the secrets that you wish to unlock will reveal themselves. Trusting is an essential step in realizing your full potential as a healer. Give yourself permission to daydream about your powers. Make positive statements to yourself such as, "I can heal. I have abilities beyond my immediate awareness and long to know them. I am excited about the possibility of uncovering knowledge I didn't know I had." Positive statements like these will help you create a baseline of trust deep within.

Healing Power Comes From:
- A mental atmosphere conducive to healing
- Ownership of power and a foundation of trust
- An innocent heart
- A perceptive mind
- Focused thought and intention

- Energetic and inspired action
- Belief in yourself and your inherited healing wisdom
- Enjoyment of the inner journey as much as the outer results
- Balancing your days and integrating your efforts to heal
- A developing relationship with your greater self

These are subtle dynamics, which, when cultivated and practiced, will facilitate your power. Now that you have unveiled and begun to integrate your beast, she can be directed alongside your beauty. Her fierce, passionate energy will be of assistance as you try out these tools.

❧ *Exercise:* ☙
Unleash Your Healing Power

We feel most powerful when we are prepared for special occurrences in our lives, when we look forward to the rewards of love with patience. True power always comes from within. When we learn to trust this fact and focus our energies inward, in time the benefits begin to manifest outwardly.

This exercise has been designed to assist you in facilitating your power and healing with your mate. Start from where you are, by assessing your current stand regarding power.

- I feel most powerful when I...
- What I want most from using my power is...
- I hold back my power because...
- What I am most afraid of is...
- When I am faced with change, I always...
- What I would like to have more power over this moment is...
- A baby step I could take in that direction would be...
- The worst thing that could happen to me if I took a step forward would be...
- The best thing that could happen to me if I took a step forward would be...

- By not risking change I compromise...
- What I want most out of each moment is...

♥ **Heart Prayer:** My prescription for healing is courage. I believe in my capacity to change things for the better.

Design a Healing Plan

It is now time to design a healing plan of action. Whether you stay in the relationship or leave, it is important to focus on healing the past and moving forward. With a plan, what you crave becomes reality.

If you were an architect, you would sit down at a desk and begin to draw shapes of many kinds and dimensions, delineating solid and open spaces and eventually filling in the details of an architectural plan — a blueprint that could be readily executed. A whole new dimension of your spiritual life will open through your willingness to develop a plan for carrying out these principles of healing.

✍ *Exercise:* ✌
Focus Your Healing Powers

Start this way:
- Identify one specific thing you need to heal.
- Pinpoint what has kept you from taking action. Release it!
- Write down one quality that will help you heal this particular dimension of your life. Be honest with yourself about what you really must do to get "unstuck." Do you need to free yourself of guilt? Cultivate more self-respect? Do you need to be more honest, forgiving, expressive, unconditional, accepting, directive or trusting?

(continued)

As each new issue emerges in your relationship, come back to the this exercise and do it again.

♥ **Heart Prayer:** One small step is a big deal. I appreciate every little thing I do to fulfill my dreams of healing.

Your plan will bring your healing powers into focus, laying a foundation and giving direction to your efforts. Spiritual esteem is not something you earn — you already have it. There, beneath the endless mental chatter, is a golden thread of loving consciousness that weaves all of your ideas together.

To create a mental atmosphere conducive to healing, you must embrace the idea that your suffering has served as a catalyst to get you to this space. Suffering can never take you to the places in your mind that have unlimited healing potential. Keep it in the background, tucked away in a treasure chest with a golden lock on it. Open the chest only when you examine the details of your process.

Now you are free to experience a mental atmosphere filled with vibrations — private sounds of harmonious nature that seduce you into loving. This atmosphere is weightless, illumined by the beauty that pervades both inner and outer worlds. If the outside world changes, if a storm blows in and thunder and lightning strike, your atmosphere remains calm, even though you are vigorously challenged to lock up the doors and windows, sealing yourself off from the wrath of negativity.

❧ *Exercise:* ❧
Create a Healing Atmosphere

To create an atmosphere conducive to healing:
• Flood your mind with golden light.

- Out of the light, pull a thread and weave it into the issue that needs to be healed.
- Place the issue in the center of the light. Surround it with infinite love.
- Leave the issue there. Regularly tend to it by acknowledging its value in your growth process.

This simple shift in awareness will help you accumulate the knowledge to which all of the great healing masters are attuned. It is the intelligence of one mind, a universal mind. Take yourself beyond human struggles and utilize the spiritual dimension devoid of words. Try it out, trust it, and be patient.

When you begin to see changes, know that your spiritual esteem is building. You are stepping into uncompromising love. It is as though your hand were being held by a guiding force that directs and leads you to new places. Your partnership will take on a different visage. You will never be let down, hurt or betrayed. Your new alliance will take you into unlimited realms of tranquillity, creativity, and joy.

♥ **Heart Prayer:** The healing power I possess is beyond what I now know. No difficulty or challenge will outshine my creative intelligence as long as I trust in it.

Detach Yourself from Outcome

In order to accomplish this goal, you must see clearly the two lives that you are living. One life is physical, the other spiritual. The physical life is obvious. Your body needs to be nourished by food, and kept active, warm and safe. The spiritual life is exactly the same, except that it surrounds the physical world. It encompasses what you see, hear, and feel. In the last exercise, you created a mental atmosphere conducive to healing and placed an issue inside that atmosphere. This is a very similar process, except that now you are placing your entire physical being with all of your emotions inside the golden light. Focus on your present reality and realize that no matter what influences occur in your life, you exist in a realm where nothing can harm you. You are already detached in some ways from the things that others do. This may seem rather extreme, but it is far more serviceable than being at cause and effect. "He did this, so I do that." Reacting like a stimulus/response machine is boring and just makes the checklist of destructive patterns longer. Rather, measure your own experience through a different law, one that serves your spiritual development. Go from cause and effect to being *in* the world not *of* the world.

Take Responsibility

The root word of responsibility is *respond* — to be responsive. With this definition in mind, I propose that responsibility in our spiritual life means responding to our inner callings. We must listen to the voice within and respond to its messages and desires. If we release our partners from the responsibility to change, to heal themselves, to love us, and become fully responsive to the endless song of our spirit, then we are completely responsible for our own lives. We know that nothing can be bound and we are boundless within all creation.

We have countless opportunities to respond to the tapestry of information woven through our consciousness. The pains and pleasures of love will never cease to exist, but their importance in your process may. Respond to the things that make you happy more than the things that make you sad. If your joy threatens your partner, forgive him for not receiving it and steal your way back into laughter and peace of mind. Responding to your spiritual core means reaching heights of worthiness.

❧ *Exercise:* ❧
The Land of the Crystal Moon

Imagine you stand alone in "The Land of the Crystal Moon." Into your ears, the atmosphere whispers ideas about new ways to love. You listen quietly. An idea takes shape concerning your next loving move with your partner. Without any attachment, see it happening. The presence of the moon adds mystery. It lights a path before you. Where it leads is unknown. Follow the path, being open to what comes next. Doubt, mistrust, or fear do not live here — true healing power does. Respond only to that which serves in love.

An Innocent Heart

In the story *Beauty and the Beast,* Beauty is very innocent. She is unaware of the power that comes from her innocence, yet she enters the Beast's castle with a trusting and open heart. The great lesson here is this: *Come to each new situation with trust and openness.* This is not naiveté, it is a way of viewing things freshly so that your responses will be clear and unspoiled. Be open and curious. You can lift many difficult circumstances out of despair and hopelessness with gentle curiosity and quiet acceptance. Negative reactions shut the door on change while an innocent heart melts tears of sorrow and defuses rage.

An innocent heart knows how to listen! An innocent heart helps bring you and your partner to productive change. It receives all ideas and thoughts without judgment. If you wish to truly experience your power as a healer, use your innocent heart. Be loving and you will be loved back.

Developing Intimacy with Yourself

A vital and important ingredient in unlocking your healing power is deepening the intimacy you have with yourself.

You cannot know another until you truly know yourself.

You are already familiar with many of the issues that are locked deep in your soul, covered up by hurt, anger and sadness. Feeling is the most intimate gift you can give yourself. Feelings take you into magical and mysterious places. Ultimately, the dark and difficult forces you come upon deep inside will lead you to positive, enriching and powerful secrets about your life.

Lauren's Story

Lauren was married to Marty for sixteen years. It was her second marriage and Marty's first. She had one daughter from a previous marriage who had remained with her throughout the daughter's upbringing. Lauren excelled in her work as a business executive. She spent many weekends taking courses to advance herself and broaden her knowledge. In truth, she was a workaholic. When we began to discuss why she had come to see me, the answer was difficult for her to articulate, except that she said she wasn't happy. The passion was gone in her marriage. In her words, "I know that I'm running away from something, but I'm not sure what. My husband doesn't tell me how he feels. He never opens up and talks to me about anything. He seems so shut down and sealed over. I don't know how to reach him. My attempts to have deeper conversations are met with a blank stare. We seem to merely coexist. It feels bizarre that I can be so powerful and effective at work while at home, dealing with my love relationship, I am devoid of wisdom and capability. I feel empty and confused."

Lauren wanted intimacy but didn't know how to get it. I asked her to close her eyes and come on a journey with me. Here is where I took her:

> *You are walking along a pathway at dusk. The steps are well-worn; many others have tread here. You know you are not alone.*

The silence is deafening, as the light of the day meets the dark of night. Taking careful steps forward, you feel your bare feet against the moist earth. A chilly breeze touches your face. Slowing your pace, you notice a feeling sitting inside you, somewhere in your body. What is it? (Lauren's response was, "anger.") Say hello to the anger. Sit down and ask it to answer these questions: Where did you come from? Why are you here? What are you trying to tell me? What must I do to release you?

The darkness covers you now and you sit in silence.

As each response came, Lauren sank deeper into herself. It was painful to watch, but a necessary step in my plan to have Lauren experience a few intimate moments with herself. I said to her, "You cannot have intimacy with another until you fully develop it within yourself."

In the silence, Lauren experienced intimacy and connectedness with her true self. Though afraid, she encountered things that she had been avoiding for a very long time. For a few moments she let herself sit in the anger, watching it bubble up inside her and overflow like lava from a volcano. She began to cry in frustration and said, "What do I do with all this?" I responded, "Be with it. Acknowledge it."

We went further:

Walking up a hill now, sense the break of dawn. The morning whispers touch your heart with new hope. The not-knowing and the despair lift. Your chest opens up – your shoulders broaden. You are taller. You walk with ease to the top of the hill. As you stand in the morning light, the rays melt into your body and ignite your passion. You smile.

Like Lauren, you must begin to acknowledge and accept your deepest feelings. Intimacy with yourself will take you on a fulfilling spiritual journey. It will lead you to a secure, solid experience of yourself and ultimately help you transform the world around you.

The Importance of Forgiveness

Unforgiveness is a toxic barrier to healing and growth. Change is possible only if you are willing to see yourself as lovable. Forgiving yourself comes first. Forgiveness is the door to deep and lasting change. Follow these rules to achieve self-forgiveness:

1. Open up to and accept the truth of what happened in your relationship.
2. Take ownership and responsibility for your actions or inactions.
3. Reflect on the heaviness of your heart, caused by carrying a load of fears and judgments about yourself.
4. Identify how you have punished yourself.
5. If you don't know how to forgive yourself, be willing to know!

Forgiving your partner involves the same rules. Choose to forgive yourself because it will free you. Choose to forgive your mate because it will free him. Make a conscious decision to use forgiveness as a tool for healing your relationship. Beyond forgiveness lies a vast arena where inner peace, clarity, empowerment, trust and deepest love exist.

Imagine for a moment what your life and work would be like without at least one of the sorrows, regrets or grievances that has been haunting you in your love life. Yes, you may be thinking, but wouldn't it be a lot easier to forgive my partner if he would show signs of changing? The paradox is this: *You will rarely see even a glimmer of change until you have forgiven.* Your forgiveness will encourage your mate to shift perspectives and make changes. As Mother Teresa said, "It is by forgiving that one is forgiven." Whenever possible, forgiveness means seeing and feeling that the other person's affront or failure is more a reflection of human imperfection than a cruel attack on you.

Forgiveness deepens and expands the heart. Forgiveness is our deepest and most profound way of showing love for one another. A parent forgives a child for her transgressions. This in turn helps the child forgive her parents for their mistakes. Only through such an exchange can both feel the depth of love and compassion for which they long.

As D. Patrick Miller teaches in *A Little Book of Forgiveness*, "When you are trying to decide whether someone deserves your forgiveness, you are asking the wrong question. Ask instead whether you deserve to be someone who consistently forgives. Forgiveness is the science of the heart: a discipline of discovering all the ways of being that will extend your love to the world, and discarding all the ways that do not... Never forget that to forgive yourself or others is to release trapped energy that could be doing good work in the world."

✒ *Exercise:* ✒
Finding Forgiveness

If you have trouble forgiving, try the following experiential sequence. **Begin by reflecting on your deepest self, the voice of your heart. Then ask:**

1. What emotion do I want to feel more of toward my lover?
2. What has kept me from feeling this?
3. What am I protecting by not allowing myself this feeling?
4. What barrier keeps me from opening my heart and forgiving?
5. If I could forgive, what feeling of emotional release or healing would I experience?

Now reflect on your future self and see an image of the person you wish to be.

1. What do I look like? What is my emotional, physical and spiritual essence?

(continued)

2. What emotional healing has occurred that is important to me?
3. How do I feel about myself having accomplished this?
4. What are the payoffs in other areas of my life?
5. What are the effects on my happiness, lightness and sense of being fully alive?

Here are several more *inner-active* questions that focus on emotional growth with your mate:

1. What truth do you feel deep inside about an obstacle or loss that faces you?
2. How adaptable are you in listening to the feelings of others with the intention of learning from their experiences?
3. What reserves of strength might you call upon to see you through this?
4. Does your inner wisdom tell you that this is a time to reach out to another person for support or help? How might you remove the obstacles to seeking and receiving this help?
5. When have you been resilient under pressure and learned something valuable from a setback or tragedy? Did these experiences give you a reserve of strength for facing future crises?
6. How might you develop more balance, adaptability and resilience in your work?
7. Name five sorrows, regrets or grievances you wish to let go of. Practice forgiving the person — or the memory of the situation. In what way do you feel the most release through forgiveness?

♥ **Heart Prayer:** By exploring inner obstacles to fulfillment, I experience the miracles of day-to-day life. How wonderful that I can know, through the door of forgiveness, the strength, the courage and the love that exists for all.

7

Understanding the Male Heart

Ah, you broke through the cover of my heart
and dragged my trembling love
into the open place, destroying forever
the shady corner where it hid.
— Rabindranath Tagore

The male heart has the same longings for love and connectedness as has any woman's heart. Your partner's desires for tenderness are as great as yours. While his heart may be hardened and sealed off from feelings of love, deep inside he is innocent and pure. Afraid to love and be loved fully, he maintains a tough facade; under pressure he reverts to form. In these moments of confusion, you ask yourself, "Is this the man I fell in love with? What on earth have I signed up for, for the rest of my life? What can I do to get beyond this negative place with him?"

Let's start by looking in-depth at his wounding and the emotional pressures that block his ability to open his heart to you. If we operate from the premise that he wants to know how to love you, then an important step in your healing process is to be completely open to all of the qualities he possesses.

Men are difficult because their emotional wounding coupled with training in male power leaves them inwardly anguished and outwardly armored. Wounded men resist maturing and anesthetize themselves to keep from dealing with their sorrows. More often than not, the difficult male is acting out an emotional trauma that occurred during childhood, with all its accompanying guilt, shame, and anger.

Men torment women because men themselves are tormented. Shame, guilt, and rage left over from innumerable assaults at the hands of parents, friends, teachers, and coaches clutter the psyche of many if not most men.

Your mate's ability to love is connected to his self-worth. Men are conditioned to believe that they must earn self-esteem through work, money, power or the conquest of women. What wounded men fail to recognize is that real self-worth comes from an open heart, attuned to the true depths of the self. Self-worth is as much a matter of receiving as doing. The wounded male is as incapable of receiving from himself as he is from you.

Focusing on achievement rather than relationships, men learn to build their character around their ability to withstand emotional pressure and pain. You often see through his hardened heart but lower your eyes in silence because his defense is so great that there is no way in.

The Cover

The cover was nailed down when his heart was broken. Whatever emotional or physical torture he endured, the pain was overwhelming. His circuits were blown, his feelings locked away. If you could visit that moment, you might won der if neural damage had sealed off his ability to experience emotions at the deepest level. Clearly, his ability to feel the intensity of pain was lost.

Now, when you attempt to tell your mate about your sorrows or pain (whether caused by something he did or not), he cannot receive your message. You experience the communication as empty and unfulfilling. In fact, many women have confessed to me that they much prefer sharing their pain with a close, loving woman friend than with their mate.

You cannot repair a man's damage. He has to do that for himself. Unfortunately, he may be so shut down that his motivation to heal is seriously disabled. If he does long to feel intensely, he must first go all the way to the bottom of his emotions and wring out every last drop of feeling. If he does not do this, his behavior may grow even more beastly, keeping him locked in a cycle of failure with those he loves the most. You must create an atmosphere of safety and trust that allows a difficult man to begin acknowledging his pain without any catastrophic loss of self-esteem.

His wounds may cause him to:
- continually shut down
- constantly lash out in anger
- compulsively criticize
- exert power through money
- spend all his time at work or with hobbies
- insist his career is more important than yours
- indulge in affairs
- never share his feelings
- do anything to avoid intimacy
- be unable to relax and have fun
- blame you or himself for his failures
- never listen to your opinion

Meeting the Challenge

Your mate's attitudes and behavior toward you come out of his woundedness. You remind him unconsciously of some earlier experience. All of that unresolved wounding has been transferred into his relationship with you. Conversely, all of your unresolved wounding has been transferred into relating to him. When you truly embrace this idea, you will see him differently. The nurturing and tenderness you long for with your partner will come if you open your heart to the impact that his wounding had on him. He cannot nurture you until he knows how to nurture himself. In letting him sense that you truly care about his whole personality — not just the part of him that will fulfill you, but the dark force that compels him to run away from tender love — he will begin to trust you.

The effect that operating without a caring, nurturing heart has on a man can be summed up in one familiar phrase: "What you've never had, you don't miss." How can a man be expected to know all the joys and rewards of living a loving, intimate existence without being exposed to it regularly throughout his childhood and adolescence? This is why you are so important to him. This is the real reason he loves you and chose you. In your powerful heart you have the key to unlock his tender, nurturing spirit. You are mother, sister, friend, lover, sometimes father, guide, teacher, daughter and guru. The essence of all the lessons of the heart can be seen through your eyes. All lessons are about growth.

You wound him more if you reject him. If you play victim, you hand over your power to him. You confuse him if you send him the message that he is the cause of your pain. I am not suggesting that he has not caused you pain; however, it is more accurate to say that the pain he experiences affects you. You must choose to believe that his aggression, anger, and withholding are not because of you, or something you did, but because he feels this way at his core, and you happen to be the mirror showing him these dark places. You must rise above his woundedness, and allow yourself to see everything from a higher plane. When you do this, you will find yourself worthy in every way. You will begin to behave differently — from love, not from anger over what he has done to you. You will feel confident in the power of your caring heart. In separating yourself from his wounding you will see your own lessons. You will realize that you have picked the perfect person to help you know these lessons.

The challenge is to listen from between the lines of your consciousness to what he says. By asking him the right questions, you will begin to learn the right answers. If you feel threatened and allow those feelings to guide your responses to him, he will feel compelled to protect himself and his wounds. If you listen and speak from an objective place, a curious place, he will see you as one who is safe and caring.

The Angry Male

The challenge: The angry male can literally terrorize his mate. His rages are frightening, but their unpredictability is even worse. A woman living with an angry man is apt to describe herself as "always walking on eggshells." He may lash out at a waiter, or at someone over whom he has legitimate authority. He may keep his angry outbursts confined to the home, perhaps directing them toward a child or stepchild. With an angry man, you can rarely relax and let go. Virtually anything can represent a strain in his life. When stress is high, he can erupt at any time — without thought and without warning. Even if he apologizes for his behavior, he rarely has any notion of the damage he has done.

The potential: The angry male is protecting himself from some hurt that he experienced early in life. Whenever that hurt begins to resurge, pushing too close to the surface and threatening his survival, he quickly smothers it with anger to protect himself from feeling it.

Men generally like women who like men, so perhaps it is also true that men are angry with women who are angry with them. The potential for you lies in understanding *your own* anger. You may be out of touch with the rage that lies deep within you. Embracing the rage at your core can lead to a powerful healing. If you are aware of an angry force inside you that your mate tends to evoke, go with that force. If you cannot contact any feeling of anger, simply live with the possibility that it does exist. Turn the question over to your unconscious mind. As Clarissa Pinkola Estes says in *Women Who Run with the Wolves,* "Sometimes the unconscious offers an idea about a new way of living."

Don't deny your rage. Use it as a vehicle. It will take you where you need to go if you trust it. Own it and let it guide you to your deepest woundedness and healing. Find your hopelessness and sorrow. Be patient, but persistent. When you discover its roots, you'll be free. Your lightened load will sever the ties of rage between you and your partner. You will no longer accept the old position. Stepping away, disengaging will lead him to changes. In your new role, you will give him complete ownership of the situation when he gets angry (even if he tries to blame you). Your awareness will force him to be with his bitterness, righteousness, failure, fear, frustrations, denial, or whatever is at the core. He loses his power when he rages. You will have gained yours back by identifying your anger.

The Out of Control, Controlling Male

The challenge: Love really frightens a man who has a strong need to control. He controls parts of his life fiercely, making it extremely difficult, if not impossible, for him to receive love. He has a need to get his way most of the time. Perfectionism, compulsiveness and order govern his life. You must fit into his lifestyle, not he into yours. Meeting you halfway is next to impossible. He has a hard time acknowledging his mistakes, and doesn't like to admit failure. He can recognize his shortcomings, but does little to change. He hides his imperfections. He lies to people just to present a more perfect image of himself. If things at home are chaotic and unhappy, he displays a plastic, tight smile and says everything is fine. He rarely lets down his guard with you. To do so would be to admit imperfection. He can come across as authoritarian and loud. His controlling is totally out-of-control, and yet he craves the opportunity to relinquish the reins to someone who will take charge. He may even admit that he wants you to stand face-to-face with him, while you remain paralyzed by his overwhelming power.

The potential: As a personal characteristic, the need to control is one of the least obvious. You must really challenge yourself in responding to this quality.

Living with a controlling partner has one profoundly devastating effect on you: Your creative life is practically nonexistent. You may have deep yearnings to find and express this part of yourself, but doing so seems like an impossible challenge. Somewhere in you is an artist, writer, dancer, musician, or simply an energetic person who loves to explore various avenues of expression. You think that the only thing stopping you from utilizing these creative powers is your mate — but there's more!

Inside, you feel stuck, like a person strapped down by belts that will not unbuckle. Each strap represents a different form of control in your life. That the straps are securely buckled is your own doing. You have put these controls around yourself. They are the should's and the ought-to's that you feel you must satisfy to survive. Deep inside, way beneath these straps, your free spirit has been crushed. You fastened the straps a long time ago, as a means to survive whatever difficult and painful things happened to you as a child. They helped you keep a rein on things when your life felt out of control. At that point in time you needed to feel safe. Now you feel stuck. More powerful than his control is your own — and you believe that you must have it to surive.

Look at these self-imposed controls as clues to your own wounding. When you fully understand their relationship to the present, you will change. You will no longer have any need to control others. You will have no desire to use quiet manipulation in the form of guilt, anger, self-sacrificing comments designed to direct the actions of others, or facial expressions meant to provoke a response.

You may be expressing your need to control through other means, such as religion, work, exercise or alcohol abuse. With courage, you can unlock the straps that bind you, one by one, abandoning your survival mode and using that intense internal power to be fully creative and alive. When you do this, you will move beyond survival. Then you can make choices about how to respond to your controlling partner. When you are free internally, he will no longer have power over you. You will know how to direct your life to realize your full creative potential, and he will stop doing what he's always done because it won't work anymore.

The Hypercritical Male

The challenge: He is chronically negative, and can't seem to help himself. He sees the worst in friends, neighbors, the children and most of all, you. He can be sarcastic or belittling, and he is heedless to the pain he inflicts through his verbal assaults. Some of his favorite lines are, "I told you so," and

"Why don't you listen to me?" When he gets angry, he is not above treating you like a child or even humiliating you in public. He knows what hurts you most, and will crack jokes or use barbs about your weight, hair, clothes or any other deeply personal issue, to make you feel small. What he does not share is his own personal pain and his deep inner conflict. Instead, he uses his know-it-all cover to convince himself and others that he is worthy of the esteem he cannot give to himself. He may continually look for new stimulation and experiences to distract him from just "being." His real fears are well hidden and the critical comments and behavior are meant to throw others off track.

The potential: You are very lonely inside, living with this man. Deep interconnectedness is missing because it is so difficult to have quiet sharing. Sometimes it seems you come close to achieving deep intimacy, but secretly you feel deprived and crave much more than you get. You respond to his negativity with depression. You may feel as though you are always fighting off some dark cloud. Deep inside resides a feeling of gloom and doom, and no matter how much you try to do things in your life to take that feeling away, it stays with you as a constant reminder.

Look back and ask yourself how long this cloud has been inside you. Are you aware of any specific incidents that brought it in? The mental room that you live in (often unconsciously) feels drab and dark, with very few objects of color around. Deep inside you may feel profound sadness, quiet despair and helplessness. Underneath you long to be appreciated for who you are. You don't really trust others easily because you have been very hurt by people along the way. Your greatest learning lies in discovering who those people were and how they hurt you. Stay with it. If you can grasp it, this can be a powerful catalyst for finding your own worthiness and love, and for healing both yourself and your partner. He will no longer be able to get away with his negative and sarcastic comments — you simply will not tolerate it. If his habit is so ingrained that he does not stop right away, your responses will be so completely different that sooner or later he will change. Your actions really do make a difference to him. If you locate your own hurt, your own feelings of unworthiness and rejection and deal with them honestly, perhaps communicating what you learn, eventually the dynamic between the two of you will change.

The Provoking Male

The challenge: In the name of "helping" you, this man attacks you emotionally at every turn. With apparent openness, he lures you into expressing your feelings, and then uses your disclosures to prod or trap you. If you tell him you are feeling fat, he'll find opportunities to tell jokes about fat women. If you tell him about your desire to go back to school, he'll remind you how foolish you were not to finish in the first place. Humorously, he probes you to "work on yourself." He manipulates with his provoking comments, keeping you constantly on guard and vulnerable. He seems determined to undermine your self-confidence but does so in a joking way, making it hard for you to retort in anger. In reality, he is deeply fearful that you will discover that his bravado is all show. His cover could be his allegedly enlightened and sensitive personality. In reality, he uses his intelligence as a tool to keep himself in a position of authority.

The potential: Hidden fears are a clue to understanding this man's relationship to your own healing process. You may have private jealousies, envy and rage that you have never allowed to surface. His probes often feel like a subtle attempt to get you to react. In one sense he is doing you a favor. There is a force of energy inside you of monumental proportions. If you were to reach to its very core and let it out, you would feel like a thousand-pound weight had been lifted off your shoulders.

Your fear can have many faces. It can be manifested as desperately wanting something you don't have, or as a conviction that you are not "getting enough," or the feeling that if you had what you want you wouldn't know what to do with it anyway.

While you resent his probing comments, which often feel like destructive spies, his questions can aid your attempts to understand what is holding you back from your power, assertiveness, aggression and enthusiasm for life. Most importantly, they can help you discover why you are not directing your time and energy more productively. You have a wonderful opportunity to use him as a catalyst in realizing your full potential. The exercises throughout this book will help. He will respond very differently toward you once you identify your own cravings, insufficiencies, and feelings of inadequacy. Take time to write down exactly what you want that you don't have. Give permission to all of your thoughts; don't hold back. Hang out with this question until you get some answers. Once you are able to identify what is lacking for you, you have a real opportunity to do something about it. The hard part is looking deeply into your life to find the answers. Once you specifically identify what is missing in your life, you have the power to obtain it.

You might want to keep your efforts private in the beginning. Little by little, a new you will emerge and he will be awestruck by your actions. When you confront the missing elements within yourself, he will follow suit. You will be able to talk about and share discoveries that are vitally important to the growth of your relationship. Once he taps into his feelings of low self-worth and deprivation, the honesty will heal both of you.

The Competitive Male

The challenge: He may react subtly to the things you do, or he may be overtly competitive. He needs lots of attention from others, and may secretly calculate how much time and attention he receives from you. If you earn more money than he does, he makes little remarks about how you ought to pay for certain items. He may joke about being a "house-husband," insisting that he'd love to stay home all day and play with the dog while you advance yourself in the marketplace. He likes the sound of his own voice, and needs to have the final word, even though he accuses you of having the last word and "always" getting your way.

The potential: Negative competition is born out of resentment and jealousy. The competitive male in your life secretly wants what you have. You have a real opportunity to look closely at yourself and find out what he has that *you* want. Although insidious and difficult to penetrate, jealousy — yours as well as his — thrives in the relationship. Try to embrace this idea. Find out what you are jealous of. Perhaps, as a man, he has privileges that you do not have. Maybe he is free to do with his time as he pleases, while you handle many things at home. He could be extremely successful, something that circumstances and social expectations have denied you the opportunity to experience. Does he lay power trips on you, frequently citing his own importance? Does he fault you for asking things of him — a person in such demand? Do you secretly desire these things for yourself?

Perhaps you would like to be so important that others would be there to serve *your* needs for a change. Why not? You have probably been caretaking for a long time. You would love to have that kind of emotional and physical attention and support, so that you could actualize your full potential in the world. You can be a leader in any area you choose. You are stopped only by your own resentment, private jealousy and envy.

It is also possible that you are jealous of a friend, rather than your partner. Regardless of the target, your jealousy is misdirected powerful energy that can be channeled into your own life. Though your present conditions may be incredibly hard to change, you must break down the walls of your own resistance. Find your power source! Use that energy to better your life, realize your dreams, and defy your partner's competitiveness out of respect and love for yourself. Use your skills and talents to become the person you know you can be. He will find himself suddenly challenged by your strength and aggressiveness. He will have to respond to your power. You won't ask for permission, you'll take what is rightfully yours, out of love for yourself. Your life will take a positive turn. The new competition will be the two of you working side-by-side in excellence to pursue mutual or complimentary goals.

The Possessive, Needy Male

The challenge: He doesn't like to be away from you for very long. He needs to know everything — where you are, whom you are with, and what you are doing. His neediness may be subtle. For example, you may always sense a certain degree of expectation in his manner without being quite sure what he is asking for. At a party, he never leaves your side. He desires more from you than you'll ever be able to give, but cannot clearly communicate what he truly needs in order to feel loved. Perhaps he doesn't know what he needs and therefore can't ask for it. Or maybe he needs everything and is always reaching out for one form of reassurance or another. He operates like an insatiable, bottomless pit, leaving little breathing room for you.

The potential: This partner depletes your energy. What you have to offer him isn't enough. Since your power is sucked continually, you feel internally powerless. You are accustomed to this condition because you have never experienced what it truly means to be powerful. The comfort with which you supply his cravings is your only source of power. It temporarily satisfies his need and yours. He consistently looks over at you for satisfaction and you consistently accept his requests out of habit.

In order to stop this cycle of neediness, ask yourself what benefits you derive from it. What do you get to feel about yourself when you supply him with what he needs? Do you feel important? ...accepted? ...valued? Are these benefits really enough, or are you covering up suppressed needs? What might they be? Do your needs conflict with your life so much that you deny yourself the opportunity to talk about them? Powerlessness creates fatigue, cynicism, feelings of chronic failure and reduced passion. If you feel any of these things, ask what you can do to get your energy back.

Start by doing one thing. For example, pick one idea from this book that fits your situation and work with it. Be successful with it. This will help you relate to him differently. Change does not happen overnight. To reclaim your power, you must be willing to allow yourself time and reflection.

Instead of allowing him to nibble away at your reservoir of good energy, save it for yourself. Use this energy to find and explore new places within yourself. You can still be loving, but you must examine the limitations of this unhealthy alliance. You will be offering him a chance to do his own work, and to find out what deep needs have never been met. He longs to know the answers as much as you long for a balance of energy and power.

The Passive, Apathetic, Shut-Down Male

The challenge: He is a time-bomb just waiting to go off. Inside of him is a reservoir of powerful emotion, but he never lets it out for fear of "losing it" altogether. He appears completely shut-down. He may throw himself headlong into work, a hobby or sports, but he is bottled up with rage and hurt. He is insensitive and unresponsive.

The potential: Perhaps you have struggled to be close through intimate conversation, and have been met with a tight, stern, uninterested veneer. Repeating this pattern allows him to prove that he is "right." You become hysterical at times, acting out the rage for both of you. Things are way out of balance, and you feel as though you are always knocking on a door that can't be opened. You swing from being passive to overtly hostile, doing such things as making humiliating comments in public.

The key to growth in this relationship is to understand just how shut down *you* are. Finding a safe place to open up (outside of your relationship) will set you on a healing course. Begin by answering the following questions: Are you willing to own how miserable you are in this relationship? Are you tired of looking in the mirror and seeing a witch? What have you done to get back at him for his behavior toward you? What have you done to yourself that has dimmed your inner love light? What internal conflicts are you battling?

To be lifted out of this unhealthy contract with your mate, it is imperative that you restore your dignity. You are a miracle waiting to happen. Bring faith and courage into your heart space. Balance yourself by stepping on the other side of the scales.

Go over to his side for a few moments every day. Have the willingness to look at yourself through his eyes. See what he sees. Feel what he feels. Live his life with you and look at your behavior. If you have been caught up in condemning and criticizing him, feel what it's like for him to be the target of your accusations and wrath. After you've observed things from his side, come back to yourself, and see a new you. Perhaps you could talk to him quietly about what you have seen and done. Own the mistakes. Ask him for forgiveness. You'll be amazed when this first big step puts you both on an escalator to change.

Confronting Negative Traits

I bet you never dreamed things would turn out this way. When you fell in love, your relationship was wonderful and fulfilling and it seemed so right for you to get married. One day you woke up beside your lover and realized he had changed — or had he?

This is a misconception we all have. Our partners have always had various negative qualities, they just were not obvious. There is something wondrous and powerful about identifying specific traits that cause you to react in anger and confusion. You invited him in, not someone else. He was your "cup of tea" when you met him. He probably still is. The qualities that disappoint or annoy you are transformative. They'll allow you to become the most that you can be, through your healing and growth.

Each and every one of us has many traits that inhibit our happiness and well-being. If we fail to recognize and correct these traits, we unconsciously act in ways that are unloving and hurtful to others. We are taught these traits by our parents and others, and adopt them as we develop. They affect us in many ways — physically, emotionally, and spiritually. They cripple us and our ability to be close and intimate. They affect how others perceive us. Most importantly, they keep us from loving and being loved to the fullest.

∾ *Exercise:* ∾
Negative Traits Checklist

Review the following traits. First, check off the ones that you recognize in your partner. Then go back and check off the ones that you have adopted:

___ compliant	___ pleaser	___ argumentative
___ ambivalent	___ judgmental	___ contemptuous
___ oversensitive	___ authoritarian	___ in denial
___ sneaky	___ miserable	___ forgetful
___ complainer	___ self-centered	___ controlling
___ attacking	___ martyr	___ reckless
___ withdrawn	___ undermining	___ disruptive
___ manipulative	___ lonely	___ annoying
___ anxiety ridden	___ vindictive	___ self-righteous
___ hostile	___ jealous	___ unforgiving
___ cold	___ punishing	___ perfectionist
___ angry	___ obsessive	___ critical/ridiculing
___ stubborn	___ sarcastic	___ bully
___ insecure	___ anguished	___ arrogant
___ fearful	___ insulting	___ obtrusive
___ needy	___ impatient	___ guilt-ridden

♥ **Heart Prayer:** To obtain the highest knowledge, I must examine negative traits that cast a shadow over my inner light.

Turning Negative Traits Around

It is often through our most difficult relationships that we uncover our greatness. Loving yourself and your partner throughout the healing process takes supreme courage. The traits you recognize in your partner are also markers for you.

When I first encountered this concept, I was resistant to

the whole idea. "How could this immature quality in my husband have anything to do with me?" I asked. "After all, I don't have it!" But I did. My rage wasn't overt, but beneath my outer core, I discovered an angry woman. Deep rage hid in the recesses of my awareness. When I finally unleashed it's power, I felt victorious. My holding so much back had been crippling beyond belief. The pain in me that lay hidden under the rock of rage was immense. Over time I learned to give permission to more and more of the extraordinary emotions I felt. Each one was a voice of wisdom. Each time I discovered a trait in my partner, I looked hard and long to find *my own* reflection of that quality. Ultimately owning each negative trait that I learned from my parents paved the way for more honesty and healing in my marriage.

Each of us is poisoned by the negative qualities of our mother and father. Our unconscious impulses cause us to react in ways that we do not consciously control. No one is to blame. Our mothers and fathers were taught in the same way by their parents.

By unveiling these traits, by digging deep down into their origin and healing them, you set yourself free. When you have liberated yourself, a shift will occur in the dynamic with your partner almost immediately.

The power hidden in these discoveries is unfathomable. I like to refer to Mother Teresa's famous words, "The reason I became a healer is because I knew there was a Hitler inside of me." It takes courage to see the raging dark force that lives inside. When you lift it from the darkness into the light, you turn your weakness into strength.

Make it safe for yourself to step into this discovery. Study details of the paradox in your relationship. See how it affects you and how it might be giving you clues about your own healing process.

Become aware of each negative quality that you see in him. Find a similar or opposite one in yourself. For example, if your partner is reckless and has trouble setting boundaries, perhaps you have assumed the opposite position, becoming overcontrolling to counterbalance his impetuousness. Neither quality contributes positively to the relationship.

Forgive. Begin with yourself. Forgive yourself for the traits that you uncover that have hurt or shamed you. As you ask your higher self to lead you deeper into forgiveness, a beautiful healing will occur. Forgiveness dissolves anger and resentment and creates a compassionate space in your life.

◀ᴎ◎ *Exercise:* ◎ᴎ▶
How I Want to Be Loved

The more you know about the ways you were not loved as a little child, the more you will understand how you need to be loved as an adult. What is important to one person may be unimportant to another, so get very specific about how you experience being loved.

Step one: Walk down memory lane, holding the hand of the little child inside you. Go back to the house in which you grew up, to the room that you occupied. Try to view the life of this young person as an outsider, without judgment or pain. Simply look in. Ask the child to identify three specific needs that she has which are not being met at this time. Be patient, for the answers may not come instantly. As with some of the other exercises in this book, you may need to let the idea rest in your unconscious until something presents itself. It will come forward. Trust!

When you are able to identify what you didn't have as a child, you will be able to ask for what you want and need now. These are the things that really matter to your heart.

Step two: With an open heart, relate to your partner what you have become aware of about yourself. He will not use

(continued)

this information in the future without your consent, so don't restrain yourself from being vulnerable with him. Tell him that you see something new about yourself and that the awareness feels good. (Men typically become very anxious about performing when they feel something is expected of them in heart lessons, so the most effective way to relate is through your own experiences.) Plant as many seeds as you desire about what matters to you without laying a "to do" list at his feet. He will hear your heart speak, and this will make a deep impression on him and lay an effective foundation for health and happiness in your relationship.

Some key phrases: "I realize I feel loved when ... "I remember one time when you..." "It means so much to me that you want to relate to me in this way, and I am not afraid to tell you how I feel about..."

♥ **Heart Prayer:** My days on earth are filled with freedom, exhilaration and joy for I am wrapped in safe love always.

Creating a Safe Haven

Safety is the foundation upon which all other aspects of spiritual and emotional freedom are possible. More important than loving and being loved is feeling safe. From the earliest moments in our lives, incidents occur that cause us to feel unsafe. You must reach deeper places of safety within yourself before expecting him to feel safe enough to open up to you!

We all have physical safety issues, but emotional safety is even more intrinsic to our happiness and ability to connect with others.

Three important questions need to be answered in creating a safe haven for growth in your love relationship. They are:

1. Am I safe?
2. Am I loved?
3. Can I feel?

Visualize each of these questions as a step, one on top of the other. Safety is first, resting on solid ground and supporting the next step, Love, which in turn supports the last step, Feeling. All three steps are necessary in developing safety and trust in ourselves and others.

Safety begins within. Due to circumstances of childhood, adolescence and early adulthood, many of us experience an absence of safety growing up. Few of us reach maturity without some trauma. In our formative years, impressions are made upon us and we continue to react to the world like a stimulus-response machine based on those impressions. For example, suppose you fell off the back of a motorcycle when you were seven years old and broke your nose. Every time you see a motorcycle, a rush of anxiety washes over you. Every time you take a good look in the mirror at your nose, you remember the trauma of the accident. These kinds of reactions reduce our level of safety and feelings of freedom in the world. Numerous recollections like these are triggered throughout each day, causing varying degrees of distress and discomfort. Unless, in the moment, you consciously ask the question, "Am I Safe?" and respond affirmatively, you move through life with a diminished internal light, allowing the lack of safety to dominate your experience.

Chances are a variety of triggers in your external environment — people, places, recurring situations — create a sense of danger. To increase your feelings of inner safety, begin by paying closer attention to the nature of these circumstances.

Listen to your heart when you first become anxious or tense, or when you start to withdraw from someone. The more aware you become of your responses to the outside world, the easier it is to avoid unnecessary conflict and unsafe feelings.

Many of us experience an absence of meaning in our lives because we don't feel safe in our own hearts to embrace what we feel. We may look to others to supply the emotional content of our lives, or surround ourselves with authority figures to whom we turn for judgment, approval or validation of our feelings.

Until we re-establish this sense of inner safety, it remains very difficult to experience the wellspring of love and deep self-honesty and self-esteem we so richly deserve. Without a safe place to go in our hearts, a space of stability and confidence, we are unable to feel at ease in the world. If we operate from suspicion and mistrust, we create isolation. We insulate ourselves from those we love or could love. The love we offer ourselves and others is wrapped in fear. That is why it is so important to ask yourself the next question: "Am I loved?"

Unconditional love comes primarily from within your own heart. Author Robert Prinable states, "Love is a space in which all other emotions can be experienced." If your answer to "Am I loved?" is no, ask yourself, "Am I relying on other people for my sense of being loved?" If so, you are subject to the whims, feelings, expressions and reactions of those people. You must rely on your own core. Love is the essence of self-worth. Lack of self-worth holds us back from loving ourselves and others. To be more aligned with your transcendent self, ask this simple question throughout your day, "Am I loved?" The answer might change - it certainly does for me as situations occur throughout my day.

The last of these three questions is imperative because it allows a movement of energy — as if that energy were crossing a threshold. "Can I feel?" Self-discovery tells us who we are, why we care about certain things so much and why we feel what we feel. Once we stop resisting, suppressing or denying emotions, the beauty, pain and wonder of life come within reach and we begin to advance in the direction of our dreams.

We all want to succeed in expressing what we feel. Love for ourselves comes only when we accept and experience feelings as they are, not as we wish them to be. Even the most negative or uncomfortable feeling is, in fact, a source of energy. Negative outcomes occur when we turn that energy into a destructive force against ourself or others. We all want the freedom to feel what hurts us as well as what pleasures us.

On the other hand, focusing on our inner safety allows our divinity to come forward. Our true spiritual and transcendent self is able to embrace momentary imperfection and distorted views and turn them into fleeting experiences of little or no importance. When we are safe, we experience love and then are free to explore all that we feel.

By asking the questions, "Am I safe? Am I loved? Can I feel?" you resolve to find deeper truth, deeper meaning and deeper trust for yourself. This simple exercise will bring you back to your foundation of inner safety. Ask yourself these questions many times every day — whenever you feel threatened, confused, off-center or uncomfortable. Each time you ask, you will be lifted out of the darkness into the light. These questions will help free the inner core of your personality and open you up to the precious moment in time that you are living with your mate.

Diane's Story

This example shows how powerfully these three questions can work. At 68, Diane looked back on 42 years of marriage to a verbally abusive partner. She had raised six children with little or no emotional support from her husband. Examining her past, Diane acknowledged that she was treated very poorly by her father. He was an alcoholic and often verbally attacked her mom. Her mother became a workaholic, retreating into the responsibilities of running a hotel. Growing up, Diane was not emotionally close to her mother. Though she loved her, Diane did not know how to talk to her mother about the feelings she experienced. Diane had few insights about herself or her emotions. No one taught her that feelings mattered, let alone listened to how she felt. This extreme situation crippled her in many ways. She felt punished as a little girl, and this theme followed her throughout life.

Diane felt punished when her husband treated her badly. At night she punished herself by sitting at the kitchen counter making and eating sandwiches filled with meats and cheeses and gobs of mayonnaise and mustard. She often finished the whole loaf of bread before flopping into bed. Self-punishment was a constant in her life. During a counseling session, I asked her to stop for a minute and become aware of her behavior.

When Diane answered the three questions — "Am I safe, am I loved, can I feel?" — she was aware of a shift inside. She had to look for answers. She had to be honest with herself and begin to acknowledge her unhappiness. Instead of eating excessively, she started to write in a journal. Her behavior did not change immediately. It took time, but she gradually moved away from self-punishing behavior. She began to notice how she felt and to acknowledge her deepest hurt and despair. At first, the tears that flowed down her cheeks were very controlled, but eventually she opened up fully to her sad life and the pain she had carried around for years. No change was possible in her marriage until *she* changed. Eventually, Diane learned how to talk about her feelings to close friends and family members. It was a big step for her. She began to confront her husband, and she realized she did not deserve to be punished.

Incorporate the three questions into your daily activities. Try them out. They will have a profound impact on your life. Remember them, especially in frustrating moments. Listen to what your inner voice tells you. Be willing to hear the truth. Eventually you will know more about yourself. You will discover more of your strength and talent if you persist in looking deeper.

Exercise: *Inner Safety Meditation*

What triggers your feelings of un-safety? What do you do to yourself when you feel unsafe? Do you mistrust? Have you isolated yourself from something or someone because of feeling unsafe? Take all these questions and bring them into the circle with the three questions: Am I safe? Am I loved? Can I feel?

Read the following out loud in a slow, clear voice. (You may also want to record your reading on tape.)

Imagine light all around you. As you move out into this light, you realize that the light is contained inside a cocoon. You normally think of a cocoon as a dark place, but this space is different. The light moves into your cells and relaxes you. The light warms your heart and finds its way deep, deep into your soul. All around you, you can feel a soothing energy creating a gentle warmth. Vibrations of love, healing and nurturing find their way deep inside to your vortex. You are loved. Your senses are finely tuned. Your sense of smell — smelling the light. Your sense of taste — tasting the light. Your senses of touch and sound are all working. You allow the light to find its way into your depths, your core. You realize how complete and perfect you are inside of this light, as if you are part of the light .

(continued)

You feel connected. The cocoon represents a cell of light that is part of a cell of the universe and of all creation. No matter where you are in your life process, you are always that cell. Circumstances may change, images and senses at times may be different, but you, the cell, are always the same — perfect as you are, pure in heart and pure in spirit.

Now imagine that a tiny opening in the cell appears in front of you. The opening beckons you forward. Imagine yourself moving in the direction of the opening and filtering through it. As you do, your entire being seems to change form. You feel like you are moving through a tunnel. Soon you find yourself on the other side, contained within a larger cell. As you look around you notice all the features of the place — beautiful trees, mountains, oceans, rivers, meadows, all manner of natural beauty. You are safe in this world. This is your world. Take a moment to walk through and notice all the things that are precious to you. People you love, places you enjoy, features of the natural world reach out to you and touch you in a very special place. As you move through your world, realize that you are safe. This world doesn't belong to anyone else. You created it. Included in this world are the lives of the people who touch you, love you and whom you love back. You are safe and secure here, knowing that you draw to yourself loving energy, good wishes, good will, and all the positive elements of life itself. You connect with these things and bring them to you.

As you walk further along on your journey, all kinds of wonderful things present themselves to you in this loving space. Different aspects of nature and life are flowing through this place to remind you that you are living to your fullest potential, with a sense of safety and security. Now imagine another pathway before you. As you approach the pathway, it changes form. Steps lead higher and higher. You begin to climb the steps. Now imagine, just for a moment, that you are leaving this physical plane and moving beyond it. As you climb, be conscious that the earth is becoming smaller and that you are leaving the physical world, taking gentle steps higher and higher. With each step you sense your own awakening and connection to a higher plane. You feel lighter and lighter with each step that you take. As you move higher into the light, you can see the earth plane way in the distance, until it becomes a tiny dot, a tiny speck. You find yourself floating in space, but something is holding you there. A universal unbounded force connects you to that place you left behind. With your eternal eyes, imagine what that force is. Begin to see it and form it and perhaps your heart will show you that which you can't imagine with your mental eyes. Just allow yourself the experience of basking in this place. Imagine this force that is holding you, with arms wrapped around you, arms of eternal love, of protection, of nurturing and tenderness beyond anything you have ever experienced before. So loving and caring is this force that you feel completely safe and trusting. All of your needs are met in this place. Everything is here, right now.

Feel the closeness and the caring of this love as it reaches out to you and melts into you even more. Let yourself have the love, and if you notice any resistance, let it go. As you rest in this place, through your mental eyes imagine coming to your higher self, the one that leads you through your physical life and guides you toward your spiritual life. The physical and the spiritual are not separate, they are one and the same. Your higher self is with you always. Trust that your higher self offers you safety and security, continually, moment to moment every day, and that your awareness will allow it. Your higher self will give you the gift of safety and security in a thought, in a feeling, in an idea. All she asks of you is that you want to know. Simply want to know that everything you dream of will be brought to you. Your higher self wants you to know that you are loved beyond any measure that you can comprehend at this time. You are loved far beyond the reaches of your imagination. Your soul is very precious. There is peace in life and it shines in the universe right now. Its radiance is felt. Its purity is understood and experienced in all eternity. You are loved. So loved. You know, accept and honor that you can tap into this

(continued)

love at any time and feel safe and secure. No matter what is happening in your life, you will remember where you came from and what you will return to. Nothing in between will distance you from feeling loved and being loved. So just float into that love and trust it.

Once you know your own capacity to be and feel safe, you can begin to branch out and psychically lay a foundation of safety in your relationship with your mate.

♥ **Heart Prayer:** *Safety With Your Most Loving and Higher Self*
In your presence I feel safe
Where the ground and heavens spiral together.
Oh, what a love place.
You know who I am, I cannot hide and
When the clouds appear, they are only fear
And shadows of a painful past.
Sometimes,
Crying myself to sleep,
Wandering aimlessly in suffering thought,
I look for you somewhere in the darkness to
Hold my heart in your wings.
Throughout this terrible thing,
To be lifted by the great white wind
I surrender to you in the skies,
Where truth from lies
Are separated.
In the rapture of openness
You are waiting
To wrap your love around me, so that I feel
Safe
To fly,
To soar in joy and to speak
The language of love.
For there is no other
That brings us to the heart

> Where wisdom resides.
> Spending myself in you
> I know the gentle sweet return
> Will bring me home to bask in grace.
> Oh, what a lovely place
> In you.

Look to establish safety within yourself. Lift the fears that pervade your experience. Empower yourself to be free. Find the courage to face inner fears that lie deep inside the far reaches of your consciousness. You will draw greater strength from the life you live. Create the safety to feel. Weave safety into your life and live fully.

Feelings don't get in the way, they are the way!

Understanding and Compassion

Once you have begun to lay a foundation of safety beneath yourself, you'll be able to find understanding and compassion by recognizing these *nine important truths*:

1. Critics have been criticized.
2. Abandoners have been abandoned themselves.
3. Sufferers have been taught suffering.
4. Cynics have been disappointed again and again by the people they love.
5. Abusers have been abused.
6. Obsessive personalities have been taught obsession.
7. Liars were shut off from the truth early on. Their boundaries were invaded, so they break the rules to cover their tracks where they have no boundaries.

8. Depression covers guilt, but the actions of depressed people make them feel more guilty.
9. Hopelessness comes from the spirit being crushed, losing again and again.

All of these conditions require depths of compassion and understanding. Abject denial of the emotional pain that is stored in each of these qualities is crippling to the bearer.

Look to see if you have any of these conditions and dare to walk into the depths of its truth. Then look lovingly, with great compassion to your mate and imagine *his* emotional anguish. See how his capacity to love you has been extinguished by his inability to love himself enough to feel the pain of his own life story.

8

Becoming the Source of Change

*To keep our faces toward change and behave like free spirits
in the presence of fate is strength undefeatable.*
—Helen Keller

In this world of easy, quick solutions, I would do a great disservice by letting you think that building a healthy, interdependent relationship with a man whose wounds are deep is simple. It's not. It requires a lot of hard work and commitment. There are dry spells in every long-term relationship, when things seem boring or even hopeless. Many women are quite relieved when they discover that they are not alone in experiencing these discouraging periods — that other couples who really love each other endure the same painful struggles.

There are no easy roads out of suffering. When problems and their accompanying pain arise, the only way out is through. It is helpful to remember that every one of us possesses the ability to change for the better and to inspire others to grow with us. Life is a process of learning and growth.

Unpleasant though they may be, pain and suffering promote growth by causing us to re-evaluate our attitudes and actions. If being with your partner causes this suffering, look deeply at how you are getting your emotional needs met. This can have a very positive outcome, even though you may be doubting your lover's commitment to you. The challenge of going forward can be interesting and even exciting.

Your Opportunity Starts Now

Though in many ways you have actualized a loving personality, when the reality of woundedness shows its ugliest side, you move to the front lines. The challenge begins here, and there are two very different ways to harness its intensity.

The easier, seemingly less risky route is to feel victimized when your mate slips into his wounding. You might even blame yourself for his negative behavior or inability to achieve intimacy. Resorting to victimhood can easily be habitual. Unfortunately, it is also the ultimate betrayal of yourself. You will find no rewards here, only a dead end.

Are you sad, frustrated, despairing, or lonely? Take a good look in the mirror and see if your expression or demeanor fits any of these descriptions. If victimhood has been a habit of yours for a long time, don't worry, you can change. You can choose to put aside this ruinous role in favor of a more challenging one. The more difficult, more empowering route is to appreciate the opportunity before you. By standing "in appreciation of," you set a tone of clarity, purity, and expectation in your life.

"You've got to be kidding!" is what Liz said, after she had shared some of the horrors of her daily life and I responded by suggesting that she ought to appreciate the uniquely pivotal position she was in.

"I'm not kidding," I explained. "You've allowed this anguish to remain in your life for so long, isn't it about time for a change? That may mean leaving him. You haven't dared to allow this possibility into your thoughts because you are terrified. An incredible breakthrough is waiting to happen, and you need it for your own spiritual growth. A part of you is clearly thirsting for change, so you may need to examine whether another part of you is attached to the problem."

Change is impossible if you have attachment to pain. This pain is your signal that something is wrong, but too often there is an unhealthy alliance with the pain. It may give you the right to feel victimized and lost in defeat. If you remain stuck, you remain a victim.

✒ *Exercise:* ✑
Examine Your Beliefs About Pain

1. *What are you afraid of losing if you become the source of change?* Things could get out of control for a while. Are you willing to lose control? You might lose his love. He might not accept you as a powerful person. Are any of these fears holding you back?
2. *Are you comfortable knowing that your situation is less than it could be?* Many women don't move forward because they feel safe in their present reality. Is that you? Does the notion of reaching beyond your difficulties feel unsafe?
3. *Do you feel stuck within the confines of a secret prison where you feel helpless, hateful, like a failure?* Do you feel guilty in your prison? Do you think you deserve to be there for things you have done in the past? If so, what are those things? Draw them out. Own them as part of you. Be willing to identify the guilt and the pain that keep you in your prison.
4. *Have you reflected on where you will end up if you continue to allow negative forces and issues to bar you from happiness and*

freedom? If you have, what does this destination look like? What is the most positive outcome that you can expect? Imagine it in detail, then write it down. If you have not reflected on the outcome of your present journey, try to imagine the consequences. Write them down. Seeing them on paper is more powerful than keeping them bottled up in your mind.

♥ **Heart Prayer:** I place myself in the hidden well of truth, where love permeates my life, and trust that the new path I have chosen will lead to a better place.

While some of you experience pain, anger and confusion around daily issues, others of you experience subtle symptoms that do not present themselves as outward signs of ill-health. But you know they are there and you know the relationship needs to change. Appreciate where such change might take you if you dare to go! You can come out of this with a sense of conviction about the direction of your life.

Slip underneath the pain, underneath your struggle and your quiet longings. Look to the greater truths and the specific messages those feelings bring. If you long to understand the "whys," you already live in appreciation. The wisdom and insight developing in your receptive heart will prove the ultimate payoff for facing these challenges. You have the power to make significant and lasting change. But cycles of detachment, initiation, disengagement, and brave action are necessary steps toward that goal.

One important aspect of moving deeper into change is forgiveness. Refusing to forgive becomes a toxic barrier to healing and growth. Change is possible only if you are willing to see yourself as lovable. Forgiving yourself comes first. Forgiveness holds the door to deep and lasting change. Self-for-giveness involves the following five rules:

1. Open up to and accept the truth of what happened in your relationship.
2. Take ownership and responsibility for your action, or inaction.
3. Reflect on your heavy heart, caused by fears and judgments toward yourself.
4. Identify how you have punished yourself.
5. If you don't know how to forgive yourself, be willing to know!

Forgiving your partner involves the same rules that apply to forgiving yourself. Choose to forgive yourself because it will free you. Choose to forgive your mate because it will free him. Make a conscious decision to use forgiveness as a tool for healing your relationship. Underneath forgiveness is a vast arena of inner peace, clarity, empowerment, trust, and deepest love.

The Lie

In loving a wounded man you run the risk of living a lie. Overlooking the truth is an understandable convenience. If you were to acknowledge the situation for what it really is, you'd be confronted with the necessity to change something. You'd be required to stand at the door of the unknown, and to go places you've never before been. You'd be challenged to embrace the lie you've been living. Hiding from the truth is easier because it allows you to stay in your comfort zone.

Living a lie may seem preferable to throwing open a door that leads to a bottomless pit of emotions in you and in him.

The lie is a haunting escape from an overwhelming confrontation. You may tell yourself things like:

- "I'm not strong enough to handle it right now."
- "I'll wait in the hope that he'll eventually come around on his own."
- "It hurts too much to think about being without him."
- "I'm really afraid that he will control things and turn them against me if I open up and let him know what my deeper thoughts are." (He may have done this in the past.)
- "He won't change anyway, so why should I bother?"
- "I don't have the confidence I need to break free of this stuff."
- "Where would I go if I were not with him? Who would love someone so unlovable?"
- "I am terrified of trying to make my life work without him. After all, he helps pay the bills."
- "What if he moves on and has a wonderful relationship with another woman? I'll miss out on all that I've taught him."
- "Maybe he'll get professional help soon."

The lie is not his, it's yours! Your own hurt and anger have been hiding behind a mask of depression. Were you to break down into who you really are, the rewards would surely eclipse the risks. You must find reasons not to lie to yourself, and their benefits must outweigh the comfort of your denial. You have been socially trained to accept the status quo and deny your deepest intuitive self. Until you find the courage to face the truth and learn to rely on your wisdom and feminine healing you'll continue to feel stuck — wishing he'd change and waiting to find a way out of despair. Try the following exercise.

Exercise: Honesty

Using this scale, answer the following questions as honestly as you can:

O = never   **1 = sometimes**   **2 = often**

1. Sometimes I lie to him, so as not to "rock the boat." It just seems easier. Sometimes I lie to myself by forgetting that certain things happened.
2. I have numbed myself to many negative incidents that have occurred over the years. To acknowledge those incidents would be to invite a great deal of pain and anger.
3. I have held myself back by not acknowledging the truth of my own inner struggles.
4. My intuition tells me that what I hear from him and what is really going on deep inside of him are two different things.
5. He doesn't know how to let my love in, and I hurt when I am shut out.
6. I fear the consequences if I were to confront his transgressions against me or my children.
7. I have fantasized leaving him because it is easier than confronting the pain, but I wouldn't dare tell him.
8. I have not been honest about my own childhood wounds.
9. When I feel overpowered by him, I simply shut down to shut him out.
10. A lack of courage pervades my communication with him, especially where hurt and anger are concerned. I am good at suppressing how I feel.

Scoring: If you scored 15-20, satisfying intimacy is practically nonexistent for you. If you scored 10-15, you have been disempowered and must face head-on your real feelings. If you scored 0-10, you are experiencing some success at intimacy with your mate. Remember, you deserve even more. The "more" lives beyond these lies, in the outer realms of possibility. Knowing what hurts and blocks you has freed you to move beyond the lies. Every one of the above statements is a point of reference for you to examine.

Only when we give up the belief that another person can fulfill us do we go forward. Somewhere deep inside we nurture the hope that a lover will make our life worth living and will add more meaning to what we have. Somehow, someday this person will come through for us and lead us into happiness. No! We lead *ourselves* into happiness. Our partners challenge us to find it!

His pain and sealed heart are your pain and sealed heart. His role is to help you break through your own fears and insecurities. Your partner can become a very real, living, breathing mirror for all the issues in your life. Once you realize that *you* are the love of your life, your ability to create true love becomes a reality. You're it!

Becoming a Change Agent

The most powerful way to effect change is to *become* the change. When you take 100 percent responsibility for your relationship as it is, you create the possibility of a new and exciting future with your love partner. The partner you have chosen is your greatest teacher. Especially when you are struggling together, your partner serves as a guide.

If you go through day after day silently disappointed in your lover, he will pick up on your resentment and his self-esteem will plummet. Meanwhile, feeling helpless and ineffective lowers *your* self-esteem, which ultimately leads to negative consequences in the relationship.

When you feel inadequate at home, you develop a stronger need for strokes out in the world. This sets up perfect conditions for you or he to seek outside validation — for example in work or an affair — creating even more distance. The safety and trust that once existed in the relationship are no longer there to rely on when difficulties arise. When the foundation for the relationship is weak, separation and divorce are more likely.

The only real foundation is a spiritual one, as described earlier in the book. If he does not have this in his life, you must, or the changes you desire and deserve will not occur. One of you has to look at the bigger picture and be able to draw from that. Someone in the relationship needs to believe in love — unbounded and infinite love that is constant and ever-present. You become the change agent by accepting your role as the leader of love. Why not?

Taming Your Judge

Another way to help yourself step into the full potential of your relationship is to tame the judge who lives inside you. Putting enormous energy into agonizing over what your partner is doing wrong in his life deprives you of the opportunity to use the same energy to make your dreams come true. It is such a responsibility to weigh your partner's merits against his faults. It becomes a great excuse for punishment.

Consider the example of Nan. She came in frantic one day, armed with evidence of her partner's activities over the previous week. She had an audiotape of his verbal assaults (secretly recorded inside her purse) and pages of notes on his angry outbursts throughout the week. For the first part of their twenty-year marriage, Nan had lived in quiet desperation, popping in and out of despair. Their three sons and two daughters kept Nan and Kent together. Counseling had not affected their arguing. Neither had short separations necessitated by various jobs. Kent had learned about his deeper family issues in counseling, but those insights had not changed his way of responding to Nan in the heat of things. He felt the finger was always pointed at him, and asked furiously, '"Why am I the one with the problem — what about you?"

Nan felt terribly frustrated by this comment because, from her perspective, she was doing everything possible to bring about change and growth in the relationship, including looking at her own issues as openly as possible. Meanwhile Kent pounded the "no matter what I do it's never enough" treadmill, locked into a cycle of failure with respect to Nan. Nan felt unremittingly disappointed in him, especially when he lashed out at her in anger.

Nan had to accept that no matter what Kent said to her, she would never be enough for him. Kent needed to learn the same thing, but could embrace this idea more easily if she modeled it for him. "He complains about my lack of passion for him," she said.

I said right back, "You complain about his lack of sensitivity to you. Could we be talking about the same thing?"

Nan understood right away that her appetite for love and affection were just as great as his, and that the only way to meet in the heart was to build a bridge that reached from her side all the way over to his.

When you let yourself get sucked into a drama with your mate, spending all your time defending and attacking rather than receiving and sharing, you prevent him from fulfilling himself. When you stand firmly in front of him without response, giving him nothing to butt up against, he will go back into his own psyche to deal with the issue at hand.

Nan decided to adopt a new attitude: "There is nothing wrong with him and, further, there is nothing wrong with us. These are merely incidents on the highway of experience leading us to new places." This small adjustment in perspective allowed Nan to listen to Kent differently, and provoked an enormous shift in his thinking as well. The tension between them lessened and his eruptions of rage registered farther and farther apart. Nan learned to tame her judge, freeing Kent from the ridicule and criticism he had known since childhood.

Being acutely aware of your situation is a very healthy thing. You must come from a position of strength rather than weakness. If he is verbally abusing you, get help! You are either pursuing events or events are pursuing you. Move forward in some way. Love yourself enough to realize that you don't have to keep reacting. You can act — you can effect change!

Don't lower your expectations, just change them!

First and foremost, you need to know that you deserve a fulfilling love relationship. By taming your judge, you will bring yourself into a position of strength and will cease operating from weakness. When you are solid, nonreactive, and loving, any communication you deliver will be heard. You don't have power over him, only over yourself. Share your observations of what appears to you to be negative behavior. You owe it to yourself to be honest.

Tame your judge by stepping back from the whole situation. Think things through and be willing to understand your own needs concerning love. This is the highest road you can take in responding to a wounded man. Appreciate the challenge — realize your potential for growth and transformation.

Breaking the Seal on the Male Heart

The wounded male psyche requires a cover, a face to show to the world. Men use this cover to shield themselves from the emotional attacks of other men, to rank one another in the male hierarchy and to direct their energy to achieve particular goals. A cover is an important functional part of the male psyche. An abrupt loss of his cover, through unexpected illness, a business setback, or the break-up of a marriage, can plunge a man into despair. The problem with the male cover is that men invest so much of themselves in sustaining it that they become cut off from their own inner power source — love. The cover becomes warped by inner rage, fear, shame, or guilt that the man buries and ignores. You must understand your man's unique cover and lovingly begin to commune with him at the level of deeper feelings, without causing him to panic, lose face and withdraw. You must elicit information about his cover without his knowing about it.

Be willing to tell your mate more about yourself and what you see as "your issues." Discuss with him your conclusions, how you reached them, and how you finally recognized that you failed yourself in some way. For example, I disclosed to my husband that one of the reasons I was attracted to him in the first place was that he was smooth with women. My early experiences of love brought me to that place. I had seen the same quality in my father. This was what I knew, what I learned at a very young age, perhaps six or seven. This was how I viewed love.

By disclosing your deeper feelings about such issues, you present your mate with no choice but to look at his own deeper feelings. In the process, you create a safer place in which to know and understand the issues between you. After you offer this information, let it go. Allow these disclosures to do their work subconsciously. They will return to consciousness when you are ready to understand more about them. For now, release them — for him and for yourself.

✂️ Exercise: ✂️
Tender Conversation

Have your mate ask you these questions about wounding. Listening to your answers will help him know and understand you, and will lessen the likelihood of his feeling threatened when he answers them himself. Try writing the questions out on a piece of paper to make the process appear less contrived. If it feels right to ask him the questions first, trust that feeling, but do not have expectations concerning the outcome. There are no right or wrong answers. See this as an experiment in utilizing your heart's power.

1. What is the very first memory you have of feeling separate from someone you love?
2. What kind of father did you want your dad to be?
3. What kind of mother did you want your mom to be?
4. Was there a time when you were little that you remember feeling really scared or alone?
5. Do you remember feeling like you didn't quite measure up? What happened?
6. Do you have any pain or confusion associated with the traditions in your family?
7. Is there something or someone you loved and lost, and never really cried about?
8. Did your dad have any emotional contact with you? Did he talk with you and tell you how he felt?
9. Do you have any strange sexual memories from childhood?
10. Do you remember feeling excited, joyful or enthusiastic about something and being "shot down" by someone?

Notice that none of these questions, when he asks you, will threaten his heart. They are all about you and your heart. Be sure to stick to what is asked, or you might broach subjects that threaten his sense of safety with you.

♥ **Heart Prayer:** The love I need is waiting for me. I have compassion, and trust my creative intelligence to bring me many gifts.

When you and your partner have successfully completed the "Tender Conversation" exercise, you are ready for the next level of communication. You have been talking about wounds from the past. Now, begin to examine the scars and open wounds in your relationship. Remember to harness your feelings of safety and being loved. As you open up conversation about difficult issues in your relationship you'll need to keep going back to this foundation of safety and trust, giving yourself permission to speak about your struggles. *Use the following checklist for effective communication.*

1. Ask that he just listen and not interject.
2. Describe a situation in your relationship that troubles you. Let him know that you take responsibility for your part in allowing it to happen. Use "I feel" to describe what is going on deep inside you.
3. Let him know that he doesn't have to do anything except take in all that you say. You are not looking for a solution today. (He'll feel relieved because you let him off the hook.)
4. Thank him for being patient with you. Tell him how much it means to you that he is a good listener.
5. Ask that he wait 15 minutes before telling you how he views the situation so that he can better digest what you said. (This also prevents harsh confrontation.)
6. When it is his turn, open yourself up as fully as you can. Listen effectively. Be patient and let him complete all of his thoughts.
7. Do the same for him - wait 15 minutes before you communicate back.

This may seem like a tedious and elementary way to communicate, but I assure you, it's easier said than done. Over time you'll get better at it, and won't have to wait 15 minutes before responding.

None of the issues that you are dealing with on a daily basis is easy. In my early years as a counselor, I was captivated by the New Age view of a relationship as a "dance." Now I have consigned that analogy to the same shelf as the Prince Charming myth. If a relationship is a dance, then living with a wounded man is like dancing with an elephant. Similarly, breaking the seal that surrounds the male heart can be like trying to break open an almond with your bare hands. Without the proper tools, you will have considerable difficulty accessing the delicious fruit inside.

The tools you need for this task are contained within the power of your love. Giving him what you want for yourself is one way to use this healing power. Because many of us have been hurt, we tend to focus secretly on how men fail us again and again. He picks up this psychic message and is drawn into the same despair (in a different way) that you are feeling. I call this the *cycle of defeat*. The seal on his heart will remain airtight unless you can find a way to break free from this negative focus. He won't want to open his heart to you if he is worried about failing you again. Start by owning the fact that you have put this fear on him. He will respond to you positively if you have the courage to challenge your beliefs about him. What you believe to be true comes true. If you believe he will continue to disappoint you and stay sealed over, that is exactly what will happen. On the other hand, if you believe in the power of your love, you will find creative ways to harness the good energy in your relationship and use it to produce greater intimacy.

Guidelines for Creating Positive Energy

1. If you are in the habit of seeing him as a failure, you must begin to work on your habitual thinking, no matter how justified you may feel by his betrayals.

2. Admire him for his strengths; do not focus on his weaknesses.

3. Show him what it is like to expose oneself by sharing the ways in which you have been hurt. Show him that you trust him with your feelings. This will reinforce the idea that he can trust you with his feelings, too.

4. Never expect anything in return. When it comes to self-improvement, he is not on your time frame, but his own.

5. Tell him what you want from him but don't demand it. Give him ideas and let those ideas do their own work in their own time.

6. He is sealed off from you to protect himself from hurt. When he projects his negative feelings onto you, he is projecting his hurt. You do not have to take it on. Learn to witness rather than participate in his protective and projecting behaviors.

7. Defensiveness, silence, bitterness, ridicule, quiet despair, loneliness, and daily regret will not nurture and support change. If you feel any of these or other negative emotions, work to understand their deep nature and the significance they have for your own growth. Do not make them all his doing.

8. Practice loving confrontation. Pick your ground. Always tell him that you wish to be closer to him in love. Help him feel safe with you.

9. Have your own integrity.

10. Remember that his seal is not your seal.

The Door of Change

I often hear women relate how much they have worked on themselves and tried to speed up growth in their relationship through counseling and seminars. They feel angry and frustrated that their men have not cared enough about the relationship to go to counseling as well. Although these women are actively pursuing change, they still need to make a very important shift. Real change will not take place in their relationship until they change. If you are in a similar situation, I want to help you come to the door of change. The thing *you* must do is walk through.

Living with another human being requires constant learning. If you repeatedly give yourself unconditionally to a man who has difficulty giving back to you, you may feel that it is unfair of me to suggest that the key to renewal in the relationship is your growth and your learning. Nevertheless, that is exactly the case. As a first step in facilitating growth in your relationship, I do ask that you go deeply within your soul to identify your own needs.

Many of my clients initially resent my injunction concerning the primacy of their growth. "Ed is the blockhead," explained Barbara. "He's the one who is so tense that he can't act like a human being. I've put up with him for 23 years, and I've given him more than he knows and certainly more than he appreciates. Why is it always up to me?"

As a twice-married mother of two grown men and a teenage girl — a working mom throughout both marriages — I understand the resentment about shouldering another responsibility. Women often bear disproportionate responsibility for the emotional well-being of the family. Nor is it fair that change in a relationship requires the woman to develop the psychological insight and take the initiative. Women are extremely powerful in emotional love, and that love is our intended healing journey. We are lucky to have been placed in a feminine life, with the ability to give birth to new love — just as men are fortunate to have the role of injecting seeds in us for new life. That is how nature intends it. Some women go through a deep mourning over this issue.

Living in a difficult relationship is a choice you make every day. You can let the martyr in you grieve that there is no way out and that you must endure endless hardships. You can be the eternal victim of circumstances, or you can bring comfort and wholeness to your heart by simply acknowledging the fact that, yes, you do choose the challenge and the benefits of growth. You can really accept what you have now and become energized through unconditional love. Your relationship can either lock you into inertia or serve as a catalyst for change.

Many women resent the challenge of living with a difficult mate because they fear being like their mothers. In this age of so-called female independence, many women resent and belittle their mothers for having put up with what the daughters perceive as unsatisfactory and demeaning relationships. Yet, who are we to judge? We are all moving along at our own rate of growth.

What too many women fail to appreciate is their mother's commitment — her courage in staying in the relationship to raise a family. For many years, I was frustrated and upset with my mother because it seemed she stayed with my father solely out of resignation. Only recently have I begun to appreciate that she endured life with a difficult male because she was not ready to face the world alone. Her fears overwhelmed her. She also had a need to keep her large family intact. For this I respect her — she had a right to choose this path.

Staying in a relationship with a wounded male does not mean you must remain emotionally crippled and stuck in despair. In no way am I an advocate of suffering and sacrifice; however, if you choose to stay in a relationship with a wounded man, do so with complete awareness — not because you have to, but because you choose to.

French author and literary critic Marcel Proust wrote, "The real voyage of discovery lies not in finding new landscapes but in having new eyes." This maxim is a fitting guide to living with a wounded and difficult male. During what may be a dark period in your life, the most valuable step you can take is to find the power to see with all the inner light of your caring heart. A new light deep within your soul will give you the power to face change head on and turn your relationship around, not with rage and defiance, but with courage, love and wisdom. The more you know, the more powerful you are!

Courage is the ability to take conscious joyful action.

When you feel consummate joy, your will extends through and out from your heart. The light-filled force within will never fail you. It will always give you exactly what you want and need in your life! If you trust it and embrace the challenge of your own growth, you will discover greater satisfaction in your relationship than you have ever known before.

◈ *Exercise:* ◈
Come Back with Love

You are so powerful and wise that your ability to change your life is without limitation. When your love partner is sealed over, angry, or hurt, and you in turn experience obvious conflict and emptiness, change the energy by stepping back for a moment to see yourself in your golden healing glow. Find the courage to face him with a different you, one that resists the temptation to slip into anger and hurt, and instead displays a curious and tender side.

Say to yourself "Come back with love," like a chant or mantra. Hold this idea until you are ready to respond. When you place yourself in this loving realm, you suspend judgment and set your mind in a direction of healing energy. You will find truthful words that bring greater harmony to the moment.

You might ask, "Have I offended you?" Give him nothing to rub up against in you or in him and, ultimately, his hardened heart will soften and he will feel safe. Whether he responds or accepts you in the moment is unimportant, for you will have tapped your healing energy to redirect both of you toward communion.

♥ **Heart Prayer:** My creative life will take me anywhere I care to go. My ability to heal is far greater than my imagination can conceive.

9

Rewriting Your Story of Love

We all live in suspense, from day to day, from hour to hour.
In other words, we are the hero of our own story.
—Mary McCarthy

Imagine changing your tale of love. Imagine that you finally create the kind of relationship you want and need. Suddenly, your deepest desire for open, intimate, trusting, safe, committed and honest love is part of your daily experience.

One of the most important aspects of change is permission. The simple words that you feed your thought processes — words like "I can change, and am changing, my story of love" represent potent parts of the process. Planting the seeds of these thoughts in your mind can work miracles.

Many women with no willpower to change have at some time gone through an experience in which their will was broken. If you find yourself without willpower, look back and try to discover the incident that took it away. Pay particular attention to the period around age ten. Desire to know, and the answer will appear.

Laura described to me how her will was crushed at age eight. Her mother forced her to remain in her room for an entire day just to keep her out of the way. Every time Laura tried to exert her will and leave the bedroom to go play, her mother crushed her desire by threatening that her father would spank her when he came home.

Laura married a man who kept her will crushed just like her mother had. The one thing she had always wanted was to go back to school and get a degree. When she attempted to register at college, her husband made it nearly impossible. He belittled her idea, kept her busy helping him, and even broke his leg just after she started classes. When Laura made the connection between her husband's control and her mother's, everything started to change. She went back to school at age 66 and not only completed her degree, but graduated with honors. Out of the love she had for herself, Laura dared to fulfill her dreams. Of course, her partner resisted, but she no longer responded to his manipulations.

The paralyzing hurt, anger and frustration you encounter living with a wounded man must be internalized. You need these emotions to grow. As you blend with them, your story will change and you will experience self-realization.

Inspiration and strength come from acknowledging and accepting the lessons you have chosen for your spiritual evolution. If you resist them, these lessons will persist. The particular violations your partner perpetrates are exactly the things that will lead you to your core. Fortunately, no matter how severely a man may violate you, he cannot penetrate the spiritual core of your womanhood, because that deepest part of you is the fountainhead of your own creative intelligence. It is your reservoir of pure love. If you have the courage to let go and discover, you will find the strength to change. Great happiness lies not in what you do "out there," but in what you discover within.

When I allow myself to be open all the way into the future and imagine the possibilities, amazing things happen. This dream is an example:

The Blue Pearl Dream

I had been thinking a lot about romantic love. After many years in what felt like a survival mode, I gave myself permission to be freer and more open in my relationship with my husband. I consciously injected ideas of romance into my daily activities. For example, if I was shopping in the bookstore and came across a romantic book or card, I let the ideas stay with me, holding them loosely in my mind. Day after day, I sought this kind of activity and made room for lots of new ideas. I wanted to feel romance again.

One night, just before I climbed into bed, I walked out onto the deck and looked up at the black night sky. There, directly above me was a single bright star. I later discovered that the star was Sirius, the brightest in the universe.

Sirius held my gaze for a period of time, and I felt a great peace wash over my body. I climbed into bed and drifted off to sleep. That's when the fun began. I dreamed a dream that seemed more real than life had ever been. A handsome, loving man who looked very much like me (similar features, height and coloring), came to me in my bed and lifted me out of my body. We flew together up to Sirius, admired it awhile and then drifted off into the black, peaceful night sky. I felt intense love flowing through me. We found each other in the darkness and began to dance. Nothing else in the entire universe seemed to exist except us. The sexual feelings that flowed through my body were beyond physical. Suddenly, I was aware that we were dancing inside a blue pearl, way out in the universe. Words cannot describe the outpouring of love that flowed from my lover to me and back.

When I awoke from the dream, it was still dark. I got up, walked outside and gazed up at the star, still blazing in the night sky. I felt completely fulfilled. In fact, I felt more happiness than I had ever felt in my entire life. The dream stayed with me for days. My life was transformed by it.

What I have since realized is that my dream lover was my higher self's higher self! I have a spiritual guide to whom I listen every day, but this was another divine loving guide, also part of me.

This dream allowed new feelings to emerge in my love relationship with my partner. I became more loving, empathic and romantically inclined. Once my male and female parts united in the dream, I was able to experience the same unification in my waking life. What a gift! My Prince had finally arrived and "he" turned out to be me!

The dream's real magic occurred after I awoke, in my relationship with my husband. By experiencing myself differently, I was finally able to recognize him as the Prince I'd always wanted. Subtle changes began to occur. More affection, tenderness and honesty entered our relationship.

We daily learn new lessons about love and intimacy, and the road ahead looks broader and more enjoyable. I have a clear, bright vision of where I am going. Through my dream, a powerful chord was struck that will resonate with me throughout the rest of my life.

Exercise: Let Your Love Light Shine

You have the right and the responsibility to let your own unique light shine. When you develop an awareness of your inner light — no matter where you come from or what you do in the world — your effect on everyone will be powerful and contagious. Where you once may have felt invisible and unimportant, you will see your life contributing greatly to those around you.

Contemplate the brilliant light that glows from your inner-self. This is pure love. Imagine that no matter what is happening around you, what challenges present themselves to you, this loving energy is constant. It allows you to release the burdens that you think you must carry — release them to all creation. As this light burns brighter, the focus turns to love — love of life, love of God, Goddess, and all that is.

Your relationship reveals new dimensions. There is nothing to work for or earn. You already have it! When you truly know yourself, you realize how much this light inside of you affects everything outside of you. The world is as you see it!

♥ **Heart Prayer:** Stores of light glow from me, greeting the world with love and peace.

Your Virgin Heart

If you believe you have a spiritual core that transcends all human struggles, then the strength and inspiration you need to go forward will always be there. Your deepest power source is what I call your "virgin heart." This is the part of you that leans on love from all dimensions. Because of its purity and innocence, it receives love in new ways every day. The power and life that exist in your virgin heart are potent energies waiting to be used. Your virgin heart burns with knowledge, like a fire that blazes and can never be put out. When you honor your feelings and intuition, and summon the courage to pursue your needs and dreams, you will learn to trust your wisdom. The more you stand in ownership of this, the more your life will be what you want it to be!

You can develop a spiritual code by which to live daily, so that you do not lose touch with your virgin heart.

A certain kind of love can produce transcendence. Love is a series of actions you take to produce a result — security either with yourself or with your love partner. This kind of love promotes vulnerability, truth and trust. In loving, you have the courage to commit at the deepest level, and offer respect and caring from your higher self. A profound piece of wisdom stated beautifully by author and metaphysician Madame Swetekine is this: "To love deeply in one direction makes us more loving in all others."

To think that an intimate relationship can be totally safe, solid, and secure is illusion. Using the relationship to feel secure restricts the adventure and inhibits your capacity to love. Intellectually you may recognize that a totally safe relationship is impossible to attain, but accepting this idea may be a difficult process.

In order to determine how much you rely on him for security, examine your relationship to loss. If you hold on to the old relationship for dear life, afraid to face possible loss, you will not realize your full potential in love. If commitment does not produce respect, security, vulnerability, trust, caring, openness, pleasure and satisfaction, then the love you share is limited.

✥❦ *Exercise:* ❦✥
What I Fear Losing

List five things you most fear losing if you commit to changing your tale of love. Put them in order of importance.

I fear ...

1. _____

2. _____

3. _____

4. _____

5. _____

When these fears pop into your mind, remember what importance they have in your life. You have power over them; they don't have power over you.

♥ **Heart Prayer:** Fear limits my capacity to love myself. I speed my growth by facing my fears now!

Intimacy Tools

As stated earlier in the book, probably the most important tool in healing is the development of intimacy with yourself. If you consider what is required to actually transform a situation, knowing who you are is imperative. When you can allow the negative parts of yourself to teach you as much as the positive parts, you will truly understand intimacy.

If you crave intimacy, but don't really have an intimate relationship with yourself, here are some tools to help you dig deeper into unknown realms.

1) Don't judge yourself. Judging and criticizing yourself for how you feel and behave can stop you from knowing what lies beneath the surface.

2) Look for the line of tension. Daily, many things, both big and small, are likely to create tension between you and your partner. You may feel annoyed, hostile, aggressive, uptight, shut-down, punishing, or any number of other emotions. Be aware of and acknowledge this dynamic. As you look more closely, you will see what price you pay by ignoring the tension. Open up to what it means to you.

3) Give yourself the power to end the struggle. In intimacy it is very important to have a goal. Why not choose to end the negative struggle? Make it your goal to move away from things that hurt you by going all the way into their depths.

4) See your insecurities. Be willing to identify what holds you back from loving yourself. When you really understand the roots of your self-rejection, you will change.

5) Initiate. Develop a ritual to help you look at yourself. Your ritual could be an affirmation, such as, "Everything to which I react gives me an opportunity to see myself honestly." Your commitment to initiating change will help you evaluate each and every situation.

6) Contemplate. When you examine an issue in your life, try viewing it from all angles. Put it outside of you so that you may gain a more objective perspective. Take mental notes concerning what about the issue is rational and irrational, intellectual and emotional, intuitive and reasoned. All of this information will help you understand how your thought process and consciousness work together.

7) Tell the truth fast. You can probably fool others about how you feel, but don't hide the truth from yourself. Lying becomes a self-defeating pattern that inhibits intimacy. You owe it to yourself to know!

8) Know your strengths. As often as possible, acknowledge your talents and abilities. When deepening your awareness of yourself, one step builds upon another. For example, your strength in developing intimacy might be that you write poetry, analyze the character of people, or have a methodical approach to life. These skills can help you understand and know yourself, so direct them inward, not just at others.

9) Distinguish the real from the imagined. Be sure you know what is real in your life versus what you have made up. Without realizing it, we all create fantasies and false explanations for events in our lives, unknowingly sabotaging our ability to be successful in love and intimacy. By jumping to conclusions, we often miss the real issues!

Intimacy is your most precious accomplishment. The love you earn for yourself through discovering your inner workings is the greatest reward of all. It is an achievement that will bring you immeasurable satisfaction and joy. When you truly know yourself, you can find the compassion for your partner that he deserves.

——— ✂ *Exercise:* ✂ ———
Eight Levels of Loving a Wounded Man

Every day offers an opportunity to see things from a different perspective. New ways of loving yourself will take you to new places in your relationship. Your mental activity can be spent in habitual failure or habitual success. Redirect your thinking in the same way that you wish to redirect your life. Take time every day to ask yourself questions. Are you placing attention on things that serve you — mind, body and soul?

The following exercise will deepen levels of intimacy within you and within your love partner. It is a myth to think that we have intimacy only with others. We have to develop intimacy with ourselves before we can truly be intimate with someone else. Find your own point of growth and he will respond. Risk making the changes and rewrite your story of love!

Taking one at a time, complete each thought.

1) RISK dealing with your reality. Trust that pain, fear, anger, denial, injustice and hurt offer what you need to restore yourself and to heal old wounds.

What I have to risk is...

(continued)

2) HONOR your deepest knowingness and intuition. Listen to your gut. Become aware of your first instincts and honor them. They will lead you to a deeper awareness of yourself and to greater understanding of why you struggle with your wounded man over particular situations and issues. Remember, his issues will lead you to heal your own.

I can honor myself more by...

3) FOCUS more on knowing yourself than on trying to figure him out. In this way, the information you are looking for will come to you more quickly.

My focus will be...

4) COMMIT to knowing your own capacity to love, loving yourself first, and loving him second.

I commit myself to...

5) TRUST your higher self. Your higher self is wise beyond imagination. The love you crave from your partner can always be supplied by this part of you. Create an alliance with your higher self.

I trust...

6) EXPECT A MIRACLE to happen in the very near future. Allow a part of you to wait in silence until a brilliant sparkle of knowingness shows up in your consciousness.

The miracle I've been waiting for is...

7) CHANGE - Be willing to initiate change and then set boundaries to effect that change. You must know you deserve change and feel worthy.

I am changing...

8) PURPOSE - Establish as your life purpose the realization of your full potential to love.

My purpose in love is...

Whatever you are looking for from your partner you must first contact within yourself. It is up to you to create safety and security in your life. If you don't have it now, find ways to get it. Don't wait for him to provide these conditions for you. Declare your freedom to love him as an independent person, or choose to leave him and move on in love.

When you feel safe within yourself, your heart grows bigger and can challenge love in any way. Nothing in your life is a mistake. Every single incident is a point of reference in the development of your love potential.

You fully realize the powers of your caring heart as you embrace the multidimensional aspects of a deeper love for yourself. This is where your power comes from. In your love for yourself, you find all of your needs and wants and are better able to express and actualize them.

What Wise Women Know

Wise women know that tears help grow the flowers they fall on, and they know when it is time to stop the tears.

Wise women know how to sing and open up their voices to let the heavens hear their sound.

Wise women know how complex all people are, especially their lovers, and are willing to honor the highest in them.

Wise women know how to carry a burden, not as if it were their own, but in a larger context, holding it up to the forces of creation for release.

Wise women dream of beautiful things, lovers, fairies cupped in flower petals, sacred places in the universe, seen and unseen friends, ancient and foreign languages spoken secretly to them. When playing in fields of daisies, the old crone nears her death with wisdom pouring forth and Mother Nature's forces at work in powerful and haunting ways.

Wise women know they have a shadow, both dark and

light. This shadow guides them to explore the forces behind it. The shadow leads them to discover new depths of intimacy, first within themselves, then within their lovers.

Wise women know they always have choice! They know they are free to make changes within themselves, no matter how difficult their lives may be.

Wise women know what to do with pain. They accept it with all their strength, and then with the same strength they remove it. They free themselves to find happiness again.

Wise women know forgiveness. They offer it up to the one in need and send it down the river of life.

Wise women listen to those who speak, no matter how harshly and negatively. They realize that they have the power to move another's energy out of the darkness and into the light.

Wise women know that the spirit of beauty and radiance flows through them always, no matter how gray their hair or wrinkled their hands.

Wise women know that the heart is for the inpouring and outpouring of love.

Wise women know the garden holds the secrets of the universe.

Wise women know that inner peace and silence reveal both personal and eternal truths.

Wise women wake up to a new day with excitement and enthusiasm and a plan to do God's work.

The Wise Woman in Action

This is the story of a woman who chose to leave her marriage, risking everything that was precious to her. Sometimes leaving is the wisest choice.

Pressing issues in Jeanette's life divided her energies. She had moved from Colorado to California with her husband and two children. He had relocated the family for a job that promised greater success. She was in counseling to resolve the conflicts that tore her apart day after day. Her happiness withered and left her empty and desperate. She had to leave her dysfunctional, disruptive marriage. When she finally divorced, Jeanette found that merely maintaining her life produced constant agony. She fought with her ex-husband in court over financial support and felt she received the rotten end of the stick. Working full-time in a demanding secretarial job, she barely scraped through each month. Participating in Brownies with her daughter, driving her son to soccer practice twice a week, keeping up the house and occasionally dating left Jeanette feeling overwhelmed. Adding to the pressure, when the children spent weekends with their dad, they inevitably called to complain that his new girlfriend was baby-sitting them while their father worked. Could they please come home?

Jeanette's life was difficult. I remember her saying, "I don't know how to get out of this awful life. I don't look forward to my days at all. I hate living in California. This isn't where I want to be. I have no family here, no support system, yet I am legally bound to stay because my ex-husband demands to have his kids every other week and then doesn't even care enough to give them his time and energy. I am so angry all the time — all I can think of is what a controlling, selfish prick he is. I feel caught in this no-win situation. I can't see a way out."

The Conventional Response: This seemed like one of those dilemmas that could take years to sort out. Jeanette had been struggling emotionally for at least a year. Convention would have had her continue to do the best job she could as a parent and try to take more time for herself on weekends. When her kids called and asked to come home, she could listen lovingly and tell them to communicate their feelings to their dad in the hope that he would change his ways. She might also look at marrying again so that her financial burden would be shared and at least one struggle eased.

The Wise Woman's Alternative: Jeanette was tired of feeling helpless and hopeless. She decided to take a serious look at what she wanted for herself. When she relaxed and stopped making mental circles around her problems, Jeanette began to see pictures of mountains and snow. She saw herself walking along a beautiful path in the woods with her children and their dog. She imagined a simpler lifestyle — no business suits or fancy things for the house. She even imagined driving around in an old station wagon. When she allowed her mind to drift among these images, Jeanette inevitably felt better.

I told Jeanette to pay attention; her wisdom was speaking to her through these fantasies. She began to realize that she had to leave California and return to her family and roots in Colorado. In the past, when she had asked to leave the state with the children, her ex had refused. She thought if she wrote him a loving letter telling him everything she was going through, he might agree. However, he refused to change his mind and told her, "If you do this, I'll take the kids away from you. I'll fight you tooth and nail in court if I have to."

After her initial disappointment, Jeanette decided she was fed up with his control. With the only savings she had, she would take him back to court and fight for the right to live where she pleased. Before her decision was final, I asked, "Jeanette, are you prepared to go all the way? Because there's a chance he will win. If he does, you'll end up with a lot less than you started with." She broke down and cried, saying, "I have to go back home, even if it means giving up my kids, because I feel like I'm dying here."

Jeanette hired a powerful lawyer and worked nights on her own case, researching and typing to save money. She felt like she was going into battle and behaved like a warrior. Every day she asked herself the same question, "What do I want?" The answer was always the same: "To go home!" Her ex, meanwhile, assured her that he would win, that she would lose everything, and that her life would be miserable. With stubborn resolve, Jeanette put all her feelings of helplessness and hopelessness aside and channeled energy into building her case. She lived and breathed it, giving one-hundred percent to the process. If she started to feel worn out or depressed, she asked herself again, "What do I want?" and let the images of Colorado lift her spirits. For six months she prepared, hearing only threatening, hurtful comments from her ex.

In a new letter, Jeanette told her ex that she would willingly surrender the children without a scene if he won the case. It would break her heart, but she would do it. While she loved being a mother and was deeply involved in the lives of her children, she had to do what was right for her. She told him she was leaving no matter what. If he wasn't willing to compromise, she'd given it her best shot. She didn't plead or complain. The tone of the letter was strong and matter-of-fact.

Unexpectedly, Jeanette got a call from her ex just hours before they were scheduled to go into court. He thanked her for the letter and said that she could take the children. He assured her that he was now willing to sit down and work cooperatively on a visitation schedule. Through the power of her resolve, Jeanette convinced her ex-husband that his control of her had collapsed. She declared her freedom in a voice too strong to be ignored.

∿℃ *Exercise:* ◯╱⏤
Creating Security

Spiritual security — your connectedness to a higher love — is the only security you really have. When you invest your heart energy in spiritual security, you will eventually realize a return on your investment.

Thoughts for Security:
1. The truest love you have is you. Embrace this.

(continued)

2. When you go to sleep at night, place your energy in the heart of the highest love and trust it.
3. As Rabindranath Tagore says: "The child finds its mother when it leaves the womb." Be willing to leave your old comforts to find a new security.
4. See the pain of love as a spiritual journey, where the destination is highest love.
5. The soul is eternal. The spirit can die, feel defeated, worn out. The purpose of all life is to see the soul's light through the challenge of pain and grief.

♥ **Heart Prayer:** I am secure in the center of my spirit. As I disengage from my problems and look deeply into my radiant soul, a state of grace fills my being.

Become Easier to Love

Do you reach out with empathy to your partner when he is in spiritual poverty, despair, or pain? Or do you turn away, not wanting to be distracted from your to-do lists and objectives, or with the attitude that "God helps those who help themselves"?

On any single day, we each witness innumerable gestures of empathy and caring, from small acts of kindness to heart-rending sacrifices. Rarely, however, do we simply shrug and say, "Of course! It's human nature to be concerned and generous." Why? Partly because there is a pervasive belief that our darker, selfish side is larger and more persistent than our brighter, compassionate side. Altruism, charity, generosity, service, and kindness not only contribute to a meaningful life, they are more satisfying, healthier, and perhaps contribute to a longer life as well. The truth is, doing good for your partner not only feels good, it *is* good for your well-being.

Develop Compassion

One simple way to help your lover is by being considerate of his needs and openhearted in your interactions. Make it a point to respect his individual emotional experiences and expressions. Develop more compassion. Compassion is a discipline worth pursuing and a mature expression of your commitment to growth. Compassion shows your strength of character and is a constructive, dignified position to hold in love and intimacy. Your partner will experience the freedom to craft his own life if he knows that your heart is open, caring and filled with compassion. If you make a sacrifice for the sake of your relationship, do it with compassion.

To a remarkable extent, as your heart is, so is your path in life, your relationships, your work, and the world around you. "Above all else," it is written in Proverbs 4:23, "keep watch over your heart, for herein are the wellsprings of life."

In our everyday lives, we all encounter and struggle with adversity. In truth, how we respond is about us, not about them.

Exercise:
Five Years from Now....

Through the heart, life unfolds and dreams are given the gift of wings.

Try writing a detailed description of what your life will look like in five years. What does your future self look like? Write down your version of a future life as if it had already happened.

Include all the things you don't have time for now. What do you continually put on hold or shove to the back of your mind? Have you denied yourself luxuries for various reasons? Have you told yourself there's not enough time, too little money, or that other things are more important?

(continued)

Bring the specifics and details of your desired life with your mate full circle. Be sure to describe yourself in the process — how you respond to him and what your motives are. Write out every intimate thing you can think of: where you live, what your environment looks like, your personal and professional accomplishments.

Describe what you say about yourself and your relationship to other people. Explain how you communicate to your lover and he to you. How does he respond to you when you have something important to say?

Notice your self-esteem. What do you ask for and how do you ask? Detail your sexual intimacy and the special times you share together. See all the new lessons you are learning with enthusiasm and excitement.

Many avenues lead to emotional connectedness. See yourself and your partner expressing and receiving love in a variety of ways. Write about the pleasurable times you have had together in the last five years. Look at the creative ways you have lived and the things you have done.

Describe how you have come to feel safe and are able to do and say many things due to the safety and security in your life. Talk about trust and specific ways in which your lives together have opened up. Have fun with this and let your thoughts flow in a stream of consciousness. Use your creative imagination to lay down each idea.

See in detail how your relationship works. Imagine connectedness, trust and balance as part of your everyday experience. Write down the things he does to enhance your life together.

Write what he has done for himself in love, specifically noting character development. Write down what you share — and where and how you share it. Describe what you have learned over the last five years that has brought you to this incredible healing place in your relationship. Lastly, describe your vision for the future. Where do you want your relationship to be in another five, ten, or twenty years? Write with a free and open mind — let yourself experience the possibilities.

When you have finished detailing your future, write your own heart prayer.

♥ **Heart Prayer:** _____

_____

Be All That You Are

If you have postponed being good to yourself, now is the time to incorporate all of the things you desire. Only when you lavish yourself with positivism will you feel the presence of heaven in your life.

Give yourself a chance to really live. Play a new instrument — the one that you hear in your spiritual core. Feed your hunger for more love with the fruits of time spent in healing. Take time to dream, but always be watchful of your delusions. They are wake-up calls. Turn your passionate ideas into reality by accepting the love "out there" and drawing it in. Lastly, trust your power to heal the wounds in your life. You can change things for the better. Your womanly love is your beauty. Radiate that which is your birthright. Be wild and be gracious, be expressive and silent. Be distant and near — be all that you are. With love.

Epilog
Rediscovering the Prince

Every man wants to be thought of as a prince by his lover and partner. You will help your mate achieve princely status if you begin once again to allow this idea to sit in your consciousness. Hold it like a treasured thought. You can come back to the thought again and again, remembering the special moments in the relationship when he has given you love and kindness.

It is your job to remind him of what he has done for you, to place attention on the good things and the gifts of love he has given you. He will be touched by your appreciation and learn how to please you more. The prince in him can only surface to the degree that you allow it. He is not a mind reader. He cannot know how to treat you without your guidance. If you constantly feel anger toward him, he will not want to be your prince. How could he? Anger in you puts him on the defensive and does not allow for change. What does set the tone for a new and different dynamic between the two of you is your willingness to give him the benefit of the doubt — no matter what.

Lyn was about to celebrate her 40th birthday. She and her husband, Jeremy, had acquired wealth through their family-run business and were finally able to kick back and relax a little. For twenty years she had been telling Jeremy about her dream of owning an original 1970 MGB sports car with a red exterior and original leather interior. She had talked about the details of its appearance on many occasions. It was almost an obsession — and a fun thing for her to fantasize about.

On her birthday, Jeremy pulled into the driveway wearing a big smile and driving the car of her dreams. Yet Lyn couldn't help feeling a sinking disappointment. The car no longer had its original interior and it wasn't red. Lyn related to me how deeply disappointed she was. "How could he fail to remember our many conversations about the details of the car?" While she was touched by his generosity, she was more distressed at his lack of knowledge concerning what she wanted.

Prior to her birthday, things had been getting easier between Lyn and Jeremy. He was opening up to her in intimacy, sharing his feelings and helping her more at home, things she had wanted for a long time. I pointed out to Lyn how far he'd come in the past few years, and that his intention was to please her and make her happy. The gift was his way of showing her how much he loved her. In reality, Lyn was angrier with herself for feeling disappointed than she was with Jeremy.

We examined her past for clues to these feelings. Lyn recalled a similar incident that had occurred when she was a little girl of seven. Her father adored her and on that particular Christmas had given her an antique doll and buggy. But she had been asking all year for a Barbie doll. She related the incident in detail and described her disappointment with her father. "How could he fail to remember what I really wanted?" She never confronted her father, but had always felt tremendous resentment over his lack of regard for her. He had failed to listen to her. In both cases, she felt undervalued.

The only way she could deal with the present situation was to recognize and heal the past. She looked at me with tears in her eyes and said, "I know my dad loved me, but he didn't *know* me." She realized that she had the same feelings about her marriage. She knew Jeremy loved her, but was convinced he didn't know her. We decided it was important for her to let Jeremy in on how she felt.

At home one evening, Lyn held Jeremy's hands and looked straight into his eyes. She said "I want to thank you with all my heart for the incredible gift you gave me. It was so generous and caring of you. It also brought up some feelings in me that were confusing and painful. I feel I owe you an explanation." She related to him her honest reaction and then went on to tell him what had happened with her father. She thanked him for giving her the opportunity to heal the unresolved hurt from her past. She also told him that in no way did her feelings diminish his gesture, especially now that she was able to speak honestly about what happened. Jeremy was moved by the story from Lyn's childhood. He assured Lyn that he understood and did not feel let down. They decided that the car could easily be modified and talked about how much fun it would be to look for and install original parts.

Lyn felt wonderful about their plans for the car. More importantly, she was pleased that she had worked through her discomfort and turned the situation around. Jeremy rose to the occasion. He was a true prince.

Now, you might ask: What if Jeremy had felt hurt and angry? What if things had gone the other way? The reality is, things do go the other way all the time. The goal in a relationship is to keep relating to one another until something gets worked out, or at the very least until you reach an understanding of why a wall exists between you. Some differences take years to work through. Ask anyone who has been in a long-term relationship. Often, personal patterns surface that unknowingly hurt the other person. It is the responsibility of both parties to bring out these issues and to ask their partner for the safety to work through them. What could be more fulfilling than that?

Being Cherished

Some friends of ours were having dinner at our home. We hadn't seen them for about four years and had a lot of catching up to do. They were telling us about some of the challenges and problems that had arisen in their marriage of twenty years. They had lost money in business, which created a lot of tension. The kids had gone off to college and they had split up a year later. They had patched things up after a few months of being apart.

Bob looked over at us and said, "She wanted me to cherish her, but I didn't know how to do that. I felt like a complete idiot. What could that possibly mean?"

As I listened to Bob relate his feelings about Melissa's wish to be cherished, I was fascinated. It was an idea that touched my heart very deeply and I latched onto it for dear life. "Wow," I thought, "I've never given myself permission to even consider that a man, my beloved partner, might cherish me." I felt as though I had taken an important step in the way I viewed relationships. To achieve my fullest potential in marriage, I had to have this also. The idea was so new and exciting that I went to the dictionary to double-check the meaning of the word.

Cherish means to hold dear, to feel and show love for another, to take care of and protect. That was exactly how I wanted my partner to feel about me!

I realized that to let in this idea, I had to do some spiritual and emotional work of my own. One evening when my husband and I were alone and enjoying ourselves, I looked over at him and asked, "Do you feel that you cherish me?" He was delighted with the question and said, "Yes, absolutely!" My next question was, "What do you think brought you to a place where you are able to cherish me?" He paused for a moment, looking very serious, and responded, "The key for me was healing my deepest anger, despair and sadness. I had been holding myself back for years. Feelings were stored inside that consumed me and hurt our marriage. You made it safe for me to feel. Because of your nonjudgmental and mature responses, I was able to go step-by-step into my depths. You put up with, loved, and gave me permission, without blaming yourself for my problems. You never departed from your position — believing in us!"

In that moment, I felt awash in love, safety and happiness. I had come home. He continued: "Sirah, you respected yourself enough to get tough with me at the right times, to set the boundaries that you needed and that I needed, too. You helped the spoiled little boy inside me grow up! When you stopped being angry and just became strong, you gave me so much room to grow. You were almost like a parent backing off. I found myself looking at you in amazement. Wow, what a woman! I now feel worthy of your love. Because you are so magnificent, I can let it all the way in."

That evening's discussion created further healing in our relationship, and it started when I was drawn to an idea — the idea of being cherished. (Dear Reader, this is always the way it begins, with an idea.) I then became aware of what I needed to focus on, internalizing the notion of being cherished.

Feeling cherished is an attitude. It is a spiritual quality that begins with your relationship to a universal God. By maintaining a feeling within yourself that you are cherished by all creation, you bring that quality into the reality of those who are near you. By feeling safe with all creation and happy in that safety, you draw this energy to you. Your relationship to your lover serves as a microcosm of your relationship to God. It pulls you closer to your highest self.

Mental creations are powerful experiences. When you feel cherished, you create an abundance of love for yourself and have more love to give others.

Consider all the things with which you can occupy your mind. Your attitudes become your reality. If you latch onto feelings of unhappiness and discontent, you will most certainly find yourself living in a home filled with unhappiness and discontent. Of course, your emotions will fluctuate throughout each day. Nevertheless, it is far better to program your mental computer with the most positive and loving qualities than to negate yourself and simmer in unhappiness.

Feeling cherished is a product of the heart's outpouring of love. It is a natural, easy, effortless experience that requires no intellectual debate. It is a state of being. Invite it in.

Try this...

Pause right now, close your eyes and imagine yourself safe in the world and in the universe. Now look into your heart. See it as a flowing river, pouring goodness, freedom, kindness, gentleness, understanding and compassion into your veins. All of these qualities are related to feeling cherished. Your heart becomes more illuminated the longer you meditate on this.

Feeling cherished is the complete opposite of feeling rejected. Now, for a moment, reflect on where your feelings of rejection have taken you. Ordinarily, your life revolves around associations. An incident might trigger an old wound, perhaps feelings of unworthiness. This happens when you focus on your smallness, and leads to feelings of impurity. The mind drifts into "not good enough" or "something is wrong." You belittle yourself and turn all the discomfort inward. This is a very limited and restrictive place to be. By expanding your beliefs and directing your energies toward the conditions that result from feeling cherished, you free yourself to experience unlimited love and understanding.

Your partner will relate to you on the level that you allow. It is not possible for him to cherish you if you feel grudges or hold resentments. He can cherish you only if you understand him at his core, with unconditional love and acceptance for yourself and for him. He can relate to you and give to you in countless ways if you are able to allow infinite possibilities within this framework.

My Vision for You

Close, but not too close. Intimate but not engulfing. Loving but not clingy. Partners that can be apart. Friends that can be lovers. Giving unconditionally but with mature conditions. Needing each other but not needy. Physically nurturing and tender. Equals in decision making. Knowing and honoring each other's strength and skill. Tolerant, expressive, supportive and compassionate. Safe and protective. Peaceful. Positive. Self-reliant. Trusting. Joyous.

Perspective

Every once in a while, I look back to see how far I have come in my own growth. If anyone had said to me ten years ago that I would feel cherished by my man, I would have snickered sarcastically and responded, "Only in my dreams." I was very angry, hurt and lost in my marriage. There were months when I felt nothing but despair and hopelessness. What kept me moving forward was my core belief that I could find love within myself. That belief grew and, as a result, I grew. I was able to transform an unfulfilling marriage into a loving and nourishing relationship.

I get back from my husband as much as I am willing to give. To be honest, I have had to ponder how to let in all the goodness. Having rarely experienced goodness in my home growing up, in my first marriage and in the beginning of this marriage, it felt foreign to me at first. I have learned to let in the hugs, the sweet words, the looks of tenderness and affection and enjoy my partner's generous ways. More and more this has become my life. I am finally absorbing his love. I cannot begin to tell you how our relationship has changed. I am free to express myself at all times. I am free to discover my talents. I am free to be the parent and partner I want to be. At my core I feel safe. First, I am safe with God. I know that without spiritual safety I am fearful and lost. My spiritual growth comes from recognizing my true self, which is one of pure love. Out of that center I have found countless ways to manifest more love in the world.

I met a prince who turned into a frog and then came back as a king. He is my true life mate. He cherishes me through the way he treats me, his willingness to reach and learn about love, his generous heart, his desire to be with me and hold me close and make me feel safe, his desire to be trustworthy. Together we dove into the depths of our negative egos and dark shadow personalities and came out of it together, knowing each other more fully and moving further into intimacy with each new day.

There are moments in my relationship when my husband's goodness overwhelms me. Sometimes I feel like he is placing a crown on my head and adorning me with love.

While I do not have a crystal ball to foresee the future, I know that whatever challenges lie ahead, I will strive for truth and knowledge and more growth with my partner.

What happened to the Prince I married? He woke up and saw he had married a Queen. The story of love triumphed. The wounds healed. The Prince became a King.

Suggested Reading

Andrews, Lyn V. *Love and Power*. HarperCollins, 1997.

Bloomfield, Harold H., and Vettese, Sirah, with Kory, Robert. *Lifemates: The Love Fitness Program for a Lasting Relationship*. Signet, 1989.

Bloomfield, Harold H., with Poetry by Josefowitz, Natasha. *Love Secrets for a Lasting Relationship*. Bantam, 1992.

Bloomfield, Harold H., and Cooper, Robert. *Think Safe, Be Safe*. Three Rivers Press, 1998.

Callan, Dawn. *The Awakening the Warrior Within: Secrets of Personal Safety and Inner Security*. Nataraj Publishing, 1995.

Canfield, Jack, and Hansen, Mark Victor. *Chicken Soup for the Soul: 101 Stories to Open the Heart and Rekindle the Spirit*. Health Communications, 1993.

Casarjian, Robin and Borysenko, Joan. *Forgiveness: A Bold Choice for a Peaceful Heart*. Bantam, 1992.

Chopra, Deepak. *The Path to Love: Renewing the Power of Spirit in Your Life*. Harmony Books, 1997.

Chopra, Deepak. *The Seven Spiritual Laws of Success: A Practical Guide to the Fulfillment of Your Dreams*. Amber-Allen/New World Library, 1995.

Colgrove, Melba; Bloomfield, Harold H., and McWilliams, Peter. *How to Survive the Loss of a Love*. Prelude Press, 1976 and 1992.

Evans, Patricia. *The Verbally Abusive Relationship: How to Recognize It and How to Respond*. Adams Media Corporation, 1996.

Goleman, Daniel. *Emotional Intelligence: Why It Can Matter More Than IQ*. Bantam, 1995.

Grudermeyer, David; Grudermeyer, Rebecca; and Patrick, Lerrisa Nancy. *Sensible Self-Help: The First Road Map for the Healing Journey*. Willingness Works Press, 1996.

Hansen, Mark Victor; Nichols, Barbara; and Hansen, Patty. *Out of the Blue: Delight Comes Into Our Lives*. HarperPerennial Library, 1997.

Hendrix, Harville. *Getting the Love You Want: A Guide for Couples*. HarperCollins, 1990.

Jeffers, Susan. *Dare to Connect: Reaching Out in Romance, Friendship, and the Workplace*. Fawcett Books, 1992.

Jeffers, Susan. *Opening Our Hearts to Men: Learn to Let Go of Anger, Pain, and Loneliness and Create a Love That Works*. Fawcett Books, 1989.

Keyes, Ken. *The Power of Unconditional Love.* Love Line Books, 1990.

Kushner, Harold S. *When All You've Ever Wanted Isn't Enough.* Summit Books, 1986.

Miller, Alice. *Prisoners of Childhood.* HarperCollins, 1981.

Miller, Alice. *For Your Own Good: Hidden Cruelty in Child Rearing and the Roots of Violence.* Noonday Press, 1983 and 1990.

Miller, Keith. *Compelled to Control: Recovering Intimacy in Broken Relationships.* Health Communications, 1992 and 1997.

Miller, Mary Susan. *No Visible Wounds: Identifying Nonphysical Abuse of Women by their Men.* NTC/Contemporary Publishing, 1995.

Nelson, Noelle and Lamm, Marcia G. *Dangerous Relationships: How to Stop Domestic Violence Before It Stops You.* Insight Books, 1997.

Ogden, Gina. *Women Who Love Sex: Enhancing Your Sexual Pleasure and Enriching Your Life.* Pocket Books, 1994.

Ornstein, Robert. *The Roots of the Self: Unraveling the Mystery of Who We Are.* HarperCollins, 1993.

Paul, Jordan and Paul, Margaret. *Do I Have to Give Up Me to Be Loved By You?* Compcare Publications, 1994.

Sherven, Judith, and Sniechowski, James. *The New Intimacy: Discovering the Magic at the Heart of Your Differences.* Health Communications, 1997.

Tannen, Deborah. *You Just Don't Understand: Women and Men in Conversation.* Ballantine, 1991.

Williamson, Marianne. *A Return to Love.* HarperCollins, 1993.

Williamson, Marianne. *Illuminata.* The Putnam Berkley Group, 1997.

Suggested Audio Programs

Bloomfield, Harold with Vettese, Sirah. *Healing Anxiety With Herbs.* HarperCollins, 1998.

Lazaris. *Ending Your Addiction to the Past.* Concept Synergy, 1994. 1-800/678-2356.

Lazaris. *Intimacy.* Concept Synergy, 1986. 1-800/678-2356.

Lazaris. *Relationships That Work: Creating the New Level.* Concept Synergy, 1992. 1-800/678-2356.

Suggested Workshops and Programs

Hoffman Quadrinity Process. A seven day intensive program that helps heal deep emotional wounds of the past and recover the love and happiness you deserve. I highly recommend this program for a deeper spiritual experience of life. 1-800/506-5253.

Lazaris. Weekends and Intensives. These two- and three-day workshops provide tools for psychological and spiritual growth. 1-800/678-2356.

Transcendental Meditation Program, Maharishi Vedic Universities and Schools, Call 1- 800/888-5797 for programs in your area.

About the Author

Sirah Vettese, Ph.D., is a practicing relationship counselor and coauthor of *Lifemates, The Love Fitness Program for a Lasting Relationship.* She is a skilled teacher of spirituality, a health educator, seminar leader and has co-produced a number of best-selling audio programs, including *Deep Relaxation, Stop Smoking, Lose Weight,* and *Healing Anxiety with Herbs.*

Dr. Vettese has performed on numerous albums, including *Celestine Prophecy, Ayman Doorways* and a new release in Europe, *Calm Your Mind.* She has been a featured guest on *Geraldo, Sally Jessy Raphael, Carol and Marilyn,* CNN, and *Sonya Live.*

Dr. Vettese is available for media interviews and lecture engagements and can be reached at her office in Del Mar, California. Phone: (619) 481-9950. Fax: (619) 792-2333. Website: http://www.haroldbloomfield.com.